THE FOREIGN ESTABLISHMENT
IN CHINA IN THE
EARLY TWENTIETH CENTURY

Albert Feuerwerker

MICHIGAN PAPERS IN CHINESE STUDIES
29   1976

THE UNIVERSITY OF MICHIGAN
CENTER FOR CHINESE STUDIES

MICHIGAN PAPERS IN CHINESE STUDIES
NO. 29

THE FOREIGN ESTABLISHMENT IN CHINA
IN THE EARLY TWENTIETH CENTURY

by
Albert Feuerwerker

Ann Arbor

Center for Chinese Studies
The University of Michigan

1976

ISBN 0-89264-029-4

Printed in the United States of America

CONTENTS

PREFACE

I wrote this essay originally for volumes 12-13, on republican China, of The Cambridge History of China, edited by J. K. Fairbank and D. C. Twitchett, in which it will appear in a somewhat abbreviated form. In view of the protean nature of its subject, it is incomplete in both coverage and evidence, but decidedly opinionated nevertheless. For the most part I offer the reader a somewhat static account, a cross section of the foreign establishment in China at the beginning of the republican era.

Among other omissions, I have not considered, except inferentially, the motives which brought the foreigner to China. Nor have I, apart from the section on "Economic Interests" which is more argumentative than the rest, been sufficiently hardheaded in examining the consequences for China of the multifarious foreign presence. The motives of many individual missionaries, for example, whose activities I treat with perhaps an excess of superciliousness, were frequently a good deal more noble than my characterization of the whole missionary effort allows. Similarly, in discussing the burden of extraterritoriality, I have not dealt with its origins and therefore have omitted any consideration of the early nineteenth-century circumstances which might have made it a reasonable modus vivendi at that time for both the foreign and the Chinese sides.

As to consequences, I have nowhere directly answered the hard questions of what influence, after all, the foreigner had on the fate of reform movements in republican China, on the decline or rise of central power, or on the emergence and proliferation of militarism. Except by implication, I have not considered the function of the missionary movement as a "transmission belt" for Western science, modern medicine and journalism, and efforts for the emancipation of women--all of which were absorbed by Chinese society where they acquired an autonomous importance in the twentieth century. In a like manner, the standardization of the currency and of weights and measures, and plague prevention activities were in part spin-offs from the Customs Service. Modern managerial and organizational techniques were also frequently first learned in Western and Japanese factories and firms in China's treaty ports or in such Sino-foreign organizations as the Customs Service. I have not dealt at all with the foreign impact on Chinese life styles--housing, food, clothing, recreation or family organization, for examples.

I am conscious of the many additional topics that I might have included in this account, but did not because I had already exceeded by far the space that I was allotted: the foreign arms trade (which was a principal source of supply for twentieth century Chinese armies); Catholic missionary efforts (I have concentrated on the Protestants and among them have dealt rather scantily with the British and Scandinavian societies); Buddhist missionaries (there were perhaps one hundred from Japan in China in 1910); Japanese educational and research activities (for example, those of the South Manchurian Railway Company whose research publications are of major importance, or of the Tōa Dōbun Shoin established as a training and research center in Shanghai in 1901 whose field research programs produced impressive compilations of contemporary data); Japanese and Western lawyers in Shanghai and the other treaty ports (a particularly influential subgroup within the larger foreign establishment); and the activities of overseas Chinese and of returned students who in a sense might be said to be part of the foreign presence in the early republic. In one other important area, I perhaps have a better excuse for my oversights than lack of space. I have limited this essay to foreigners and foreign institutions physically present in China in the early republic. The Western ideas with which Chinese intellectuals wrestled in these years came mainly not from resident foreigners but from the original and translated texts (including Japanese translations) which were the fruits of pre-World War I European civilization. I could perhaps have considered what was available in Chinese translation, but intellectual history proper has to remain someone else's brief.

One further aspect of this essay may trouble the reader: its level of generality. I have tended to ignore intraforeign establishment conflicts and to treat the several groups of foreigners whom I describe as relatively homogenous. Thus I am aware of, but have not focussed upon, conflicts within the missionary community (Catholic versus Protestant, or ordained versus nonordained and evangelical versus "Social Gospel" among the Protestants), and the serious strains between American and Japanese residents (for example, the latter felt that the anti-Japanese boycotts of 1919 were American instigated). In dealing with the foreign economic presence, I have given no space to the micro-economic effects of foreign firms at certain times and in some places which indeed may have been disastrous for their Chinese competitors. But the overall economic effect of the foreigner, I strongly hold, was as I have stated it.

And in passing I apologize for the seeming claim to omniscience which must accompany any judgment that another's competence in Chinese was or was not "adequate."

In sum, these pages might have a place in a much longer book, which someone other than I may wish to write, extending chronologically both before and beyond the decade 1910-1920 and including all that I have admitted above to omitting and much else as well. A full treatment of the foreign establishment in China between the Opium War and the founding of the People's Republic in 1949 would arguably have to consider at least the following principal themes: the motives of the foreigner; his institutions and actions in China-- the subject of this essay; Chinese perceptions of the foreign presence; and the consequences of all of the above for China's modern history.

Although changes in the contours of the foreign presence in China occurred after 1910-1920, this cross section may still be a good place to begin. This decade marked the apogee of the foreign imperialist impact on China; many central features of the foreign establishment did not alter significantly before the 1930s or 1940s while, of course, others did; and it seems critical before undertaking an extended historical analysis of republican China to establish a benchmark for the foreign intruder against which each of the major nationalist, centralizing efforts of twentieth century China-- those of Yuan Shih-k'ai, the Kuomintang, and the Communist Party-- had to contend.

I am grateful to my colleagues Rhoads Murphey and Ernest P. Young for their careful readings of my manuscript which helped me to avoid some egregious errors.

Albert Feuerwerker
Ann Arbor, Michigan
September 1976

I. TERRITORY, PEOPLE, EXTRATERRITORIALITY, ARMED FORCE

The foreign establishment in early republican China had many facets: territory, people, rights established by treaty or unilaterally asserted, armed force, diplomacy, religion, commerce, journalism, freebooting adventure, racial attitudes. In the pages that follow I undertake to describe briefly the dimensions of each of the principal guises in which the foreigner impinged upon the polity, economy, society, and mind of China. With China's international relations more strictly understood, which are treated at length elsewhere, I am only obliquely concerned. The setting, for the most part, is the decade 1910-1920.

To begin with the obvious: although some foreigners might have contemplated that outcome with equanimity, China--unlike India, Southeast Asia (except Thailand), and most of Africa--was not partitioned and ruled by the alien powers which confronted and imposed themselves upon the weakened Ch'ing empire in the last half of the nineteenth century. Perhaps it was too big for any one to swallow, and--misleadingly--too dazzling a prize for a satisfactory division of shares to be worked out, given the rivalries and constraints of the pre-World War I international system. China's sovereignty might be derogated, but it never came near to being extinguished. In whatever manifestation he presented himself, the foreigner in China had always to acknowledge that there was a Chinese authority, central or local, with which he had to contend. He might threaten it, defraud it, bribe it, seek to ingratiate himself with it, with greater or lesser success, but he could not avoid taking account of it.

In some parts of China's territory, however, that authority was formally diminished, even ceded, in the interests of foreign claimants and as a consequence of demands to which China acceded only because it was too weak to refuse. These were variously treaty ports, concessions, leaseholds, and spheres of influence. With the twentieth-century nationalist claims that the Ch'ing empire "lost" Indo-China to France, Burma and Tibet to England, Korea to Japan, eastern Siberia and then Outer Mongolia to Russia, I shall not deal here. A discussion of ideology and reality in the "tribute system" of the Ch'ing period would take us too far afield.

1

"Treaty port" is a protean term. The precise limits of the chiang-k'ou, literally "harbors" or "anchorages," where the Treaty of Nanking permitted foreigners to reside and trade were matters of dispute because the English text read, more broadly, "cities and towns." But there is no question that Shanghai, Canton, Foochow, Amoy, and Ningpo were seaports. By 1893, twenty-eight additional places had been opened to foreign trade, and during 1894-1917, fifty-nine more, making a total of ninety-two by the latter date. Some were inland cities or places on China's land frontiers; others were coastal ports or railroad junctions in Manchuria; many were river ports on the Yangtze or West rivers. Collectively they were commonly called shang-pu, for which "open ports" or "treaty ports" is a usable translation. Juridically, these places open to foreign trade and usually residence as well fell into three categories: "treaty ports" proper, i.e., places opened as a consequence of an international treaty or agreement; ports voluntarily opened upon the part of China and not required as a matter of treaty obligation; and "ports of call" at which foreign steamers were permitted to land or take on passengers and, under certain restrictions, goods, but at which foreign residence was prohibited. Maritime Customs stations were maintained at forty-eight open ports as of 1915, which suggests how many played any significant role in China's international commerce.

At the "treaty ports" proper, China's sovereignty had been diminished by treaty in two important respects: foreign nationals could reside, own real property, and engage in business at these places under the extraterritorial jurisdiction of their consuls (and might travel inland with a passport, but could not legally, except for missionaries, reside in the interior); and foreign goods, having been landed at a treaty port, were upon one payment of the import duty (according to a tariff China did not control) exempt from all further levies if reshipped to a second, or third, etc., treaty port. The treaty powers forced the Chinese government to extend this tariff privilege to the voluntarily opened ports, but these last were distinguished from those treaty ports in which foreign "concessions" or "settlements" existed in that Chinese local officials retained exclusive control of the municipal administration and police.

Foreign concessions or settlements were established in sixteen treaty ports, that is, specific areas were set aside for foreign residence in which local administration (police, sanitation, roads, building regulations, etc.) was in foreign hands and was financed by local taxes levied by the foreign authorities. The foreign residential areas at Tientsin, Hankow, and Canton, for example, were "concessions." In these places entire areas were expropriated or purchased by the Chinese government and leased in perpetuity to particular powers (Britain, France, Germany, Japan, Russia, Belgium, Italy, and Austria-Hungary at Tientsin; Britain, France, Germany, Japan, and Russia at Hankow; Britain and France at Canton). The consul of the nation holding the concessional lease, aided sometimes by a municipal council, was the chief official of each concession through whom individual foreigners obtained subleases to particular pieces of property. The International and French "settlements" in Shanghai consisted of areas set apart by treaty for foreign residence and trade but not leased to the powers concerned. It was the Chinese authorities who issued title deeds to the foreigners who purchased land from the original Chinese owners. The deeds were registered in the foreign consulates, in effect a title guarantee which made the transfer of land more certain and enhanced the value of real property--to the advantage of foreign lawyers, missionaries and others who realized considerable income from registering, as trustee owners, Chinese land with the consulates. No Chinese was legally permitted to hold land in a concession, although in fact many did through foreign "fronts." In the Shanghai settlements, substantial land was held directly by Chinese and never transferred to foreign ownership.

By means of pressure on the Tsungli Yamen by the Diplomatic Body in Peking--a formally legitimate means to obtain results in China--the limits of the International Settlement, originally an area of approximately one square mile for the combined British and American settlements, were extended to 2.75 square miles in 1893 and 8.35 square miles in 1899. The French Settlement, originally 0.26 square miles in area, grew by extensions in 1881, 1900, and 1914 to 3.9 square miles. Efforts in 1915 and later by the Municipal Council of the International Settlement and the British minister in Peking to obtain formal approval for the incorporation of additional territory into the International Settlement were resisted by the Chinese government, now beginning to respond to nationalist sentiment which demanded the rendition of all foreign concessions and settlements. But by the development and occupation of adjacent lands--the building of extra-concessional roads followed by water mains and electrical lines, leading ultimately to the assertion of tax and police powers--the area under de facto foreign control was considerably enlarged between 1916 and 1925.

Exclusively foreign municipal governments were elaborated in the Shanghai settlements through the medium of successive "Land Regulations" issued by the foreign consuls. This municipal development the Chinese had not envisaged when they assented to the 1842, 1843, and 1858 treaties, but the Peking government had to accept as fait accompli what the Diplomatic Body, which sometimes as in 1898 substantially modified Shanghai's proposals, presented for its formal sanction. The 1898 Land Regulations, the last revision of the "constitution" of the International Settlement before 1928 when Chinese representatives were admitted to the Municipal Council, provided the dominant "taipan oligarchy" with less formal autonomy than it sought in that decisions of the annual Ratepayers' Meeting remained subject to the approval of the Shanghai Consular Body and the Diplomatic Body in Peking while the Municipal Council's powers were nominally restricted. Friction between Shanghai and the Consular and Diplomatic Bodies was frequent and on occasion open. In practice, however, the latter might criticize but usually supported the more aggressive attitude of the Shanghai residents toward local Chinese authority.

The Municipal Council of the International Settlement, formally only an executive body of the Ratepayers' Meeting, extended its authority steadily and acquired wide power of government, including the power to tax and police both foreign and Chinese residents. (No Chinese taxes were collected in the foreign settlements in Shanghai apart from a land tax--since the land remained Chinese territory-- and the Maritime Customs duties.) Its nine members were chosen by an electorate limited to foreigners who owned land valued at not less than 500 taels or who paid a rental of at least 500 taels per annum. These numbered slightly more than 2,000 in the early republic, less than ten percent of the total foreign population. Ratepayers' meetings, in the absence of extraordinary issues, were often poorly attended. Election to the Council was to a degree managed by a small inner circle, largely British, representing business interests. The municipal employees of the International Settlement were predominately British (965 out of 1,076 in the early 1920s not including 792 Sikhs in the police force) as were the heads of all the principal departments--Health, Public Works, Electricity, Sewage Disposal, Finance, the Fire Brigade, the Volunteer Corps, and the

Secretariat of the Municipal Council.   The director of the Municipal
Band, however, was an Italian.

Chinese sovereignty was barely preserved, but in practice the
concessions and settlements were self-governing foreign enclaves in
which, in addition to the extraterritorial rights and privileges which
foreigners enjoyed anywhere else in China, the foreign authorities
exercised de facto jurisdiction over Chinese residents who constituted the overwhelming majority of the population but were not accorded any participation in the municipal governments.   Chinese
living in the concessions or settlements could be arrested by Chinese authorities only with the approval of the appropriate foreign
consul.   In the Shanghai International Settlement, civil or criminal
cases between Chinese were tried before a Mixed Court dominated
in practice (not by treaty right) by foreign assessors.   The right
of Chinese troops to pass through the concessions or settlements,
though they were parts of Chinese territory, was consistently denied
by the foreign municipal authorities, who maintained that these were
neutral territories with respect to China's civil wars.

Life for most foreign residents of the concessions and settlements may perhaps be caricatured with the observation that nothing
other than ricksha (at five cents a mile) or sampan hire was ever
paid for in cash, including the Sunday collection in church.   The
omnipresent "chit" symbolized the largely self-contained world in
which the commercial, diplomatic, military, and religious representatives of the powers passed their sojourns in China.   That some
became knowledgeable observers of the Chinese scene, learned the
language and something of the artistic and literary culture, even
made Chinese friends, does not gainsay the fact that for the majority
the daily "diet," literally and figuratively, was constituted of foreign
ingredients transplanted to China's soil.   "It was the first of many
hundreds of similar meals that I was to eat during the next few
years," a new American employee recalled the British and American
Tobacco Company mess that he joined in August 1911, "a thin
consommé, breaded veal cutlet, rice, a boiled vegetable and a
sticky pastry.   English cooking--the flavor cooked out--with the
inevitable Lea & Perrin's sauce."[1]   But it was not only "the good
old L. & P." that became standard fare in a country whose indigenous cuisine was matchless but undiscovered by many of the "old
China hands."

Rarely did a Shanghai resident set foot in the "native city."
Outside of business hours which necessitated some contact with Chinese, leisure time was spent entirely with other expatriates in a
panoply of pursuits characteristic of treaty port life before the more
hectic 1920s and 1930s.   Wealthy citizens and their wives in their
open carriages drove in the late afternoon up and down the winding
boulevards of Bubbling Well Road.   The grand villas of the taipans
along this avenue, with their spacious gardens and tennis courts,
were the scenes of lengthy afternoon teas in the English style.
Abundant and inexpensive servants permitted for some a style of
dining and entertainment more lavish than the BAT mess described
above, but still reflecting the fact that foreign Shanghai was a British city--soup, fish, game, joint, savory, dessert, followed by cof-
fee, port, liqueurs, cigars for the gentlemen.   Bridge, accompanied
by successive Scotch-and-sodas, accounted for many of the hours
after dinner.   Before the movies, cabarets, and nightclubs which
multiplied in profusion after World War I, "night life" outside of
the leading hotels (the Astor House, first class with sumptuous appointments, on Whangpoo Road; the Palace and the Grand; l'Hotel
des Colonies in the French Settlement; the Japanese Hōyō-kwan and
Banzai-kwan on Seward Road) and social clubs (the British Shanghai
Club, the German Club Concordia, and the Masonic Club, all on the
Bund; the Country Club on Bubbling Well Road; the Japanese Club on
Boone Road; and those, less exclusive, associated with the Seamen's
Association, the Foreign YMCA, the Customs Service, and the Volunteer Corps) was limited to a few places like Louis Ladow's Carlton
Café and Restaurant on Ningpo Road which provided excellent dinners with music to parties of the city's foreign society in full dress.
"But by ten o'clock the mixed dinner parties ended and only men
were left.   That was understood.   From ten until bleak dawn other
ladies of various nationalities, American, English, French and perhaps German, Russian, Italian and Spanish, from forbidding looking
grey stone houses in Kiangse and Soochow Streets, drifted in and
out, shooting up the sales of champagnes and sparkling burgundies
to enormous quantities."[2]

The Racecourse, with impressive grandstand and clubhouse
and covering an extensive area along Defence Creek at the east end
of Bubbling Well Road, was the scene of three-day meets twice a
year, in May and November.   The center of the grounds was laid
out as a cricket field and tennis courts.   Foreign Shanghai's devo-
tion to sports, riding and tennis especially, compensated perhaps

for the bibulousness common at most social gatherings. Horses and carriages were for hire at three foreign-owned stables, the Shanghai Horse Bazaar and the George Dallas Stables in Bubbling Well Road, and the Dallas Horse Repository next to the Racecourse. The Cricket Club was equipped with twelve tennis courts and eighteen nets for the practice of cricket. The Shanghai Golf Club was formed in 1894 and a handsome clubhouse with dressing rooms for ladies and gentlemen, gear room, and bar was erected in 1898. Also included in the array of athletic clubs were the Shanghai Rowing Club, the Yacht Club, the Paper Hunt Club ("fox" hunting in the countryside, in pursuit of riders wearing red cowls who scattered paper to mark a trail for the hunters), the Lawn Tennis Club, the Rifle Club, the Baseball Club, and others.

Between rides or sets of tennis there were the productions of the Shanghai Amateur Dramatic Club (Gilbert and Sullivan was de rigueur) and of the Société Dramatique Française in the French Settlement. The Municipal Band performed in the Public Gardens between May and November; in the winter months it played in the Town Hall. Each foreign community maintained its own association--the American Association of China, the Deutsche Vereinigung, St. George's Association for the British, St. Andrew's Society for the Scots, St. Patrick's Society for the Irish--and national holidays and folk days were celebrated with gusto. Energy was apparently available for somewhat more serious literary and educational associations: China Branch of the Royal Asiatic Society, Photographic Society, Union Church Literary and Society Guild, American Women's Literary Association, Horticulture Society, American University Club, Deutscher Concert Verein, and Literarischer Abend, among others. Philanthropic and charitable societies were not missing, among them the Shanghai Society for the Prevention of Cruelty to Animals, Benevolent Society, Seamen's Mission, and First Aid Association. The international Chamber of Commerce was the most powerful of the professional and business associations, which included among others the Stockbrokers' Association, the Pilots' Association, and the Society of Engineers and Architects with more than one hundred members.

Schools for European children were the Shanghai Public School, with a typical English curriculum, l'Ecole Municipale in the French Settlement, and the Deutsche Schule in Whangpoo Road; there was also a Japanese Primary School. Hospitals were maintained by the Municipal Council of the International Settlement, by several mission societies, and by the Japanese community. The Public Library had 15,000 Western-language volumes before World War I. A dozen mission associations maintained establishments in Shanghai, making it the largest center of missionary activity in China. Protestant churches included the very large Church of the Holy Trinity (in thirteenth-century Gothic style, the Cathedral Church of the Anglican Bishop of Mid-China), the Union Church (early English style, in Soochow Road), the Baptist Church on the Bund, and the Deutsche Evangelische Kirche in Whangpoo Road. Catholic churches were located both in the French and International Settlements. A mosque, a synagogue, and a Japanese Buddhist temple were also available. Weeks and Company, Lane, Crawford and Company, Holl and Holtz, Whiteaway, Laidlaw and Company for provisions, furniture, drapery, millinery; Kelly and Walsh for books and maps; Hope Brothers and Company, jewellers; the Shanghai Dispensary in Soochow Road; the North-China Daily News, Shanghai Mercury, Shanghai Times, and China Press, l'Echo de Chine, Der Ostasiatische Lloyd, the Shanhai Nippō, all foreign-language daily papers--anything could be bought or read in Shanghai.[3]

Shanghai was the node of the foreign occupation of China; the other concessions and settlements took it as a model. Tientsin, its concession area under seven different national administrations and including three separate British municipal districts, counted five churches, eight tennis clubs, five lodges, seven national associations, seven social clubs (the British Tientsin Club was the oldest, the Concordia Club for the Germans, the French Cercle d'Escrime, a Japanese Club, etc.), swimming, hockey, baseball, cricket, and golf clubs, and of course the Race Club with a fine new grandstand built in 1901 to replace an older structure destroyed by the Boxers. The Volunteer Corps dated from 1898; the Municipal Library located in the British Concession held 7,000 volumes; and the Peking and Tientsin Times, edited from 1914 by H. G. W. Woodhead who was also editor and publisher of The China Year Book, competed with the Tenshin Nichi-nichi Shimbun, l'Echo de Tientsin, and the Tageblatt für Nord China.

At Hankow the British, French, Russian, German, and Japanese concessions stretched along the Yangtze River for several miles, miniature European cities tied together by the Bund, a fine boulevard with shade trees and grass between the paved roadway and sidewalks. Each afternoon the foreign community gathered at the Race Club for tea followed by tennis or golf. Hankow's eighteen-hole course was

the best in Asia. The verandahed club house--containing a swimming
pool, game rooms, lockers, a large tea room--had a famous long
bar, much frequented by the officers of the foreign gunboats which
patrolled the Yangtze.

A glittering life, all things considered, which makes it easy
to understand why "old China hands" were so jealous of their privileges. The "Shanghai mentality" not only brooked no interference
from the Chinese authorities, but typically considered the Diplomatic
and Consular Bodies as nuisances who might sometimes be made use
of but who were always excessively considerate of Chinese suscep-
tibilities. While I have emphasized the glitter, following the more
accessible sources, it was not all so simple. Life in treaty port
society in Shanghai and elsewhere was divided by sharp class lines.
A man was known by his type of business, the clubs to which he
belonged, and the number of ponies he owned. The Jewish, Portuguese, and Eurasian populations lived segregated social lives. While
the small Jewish commercial community in Shanghai was in general
well-off, the Portuguese and Eurasians filled most of the routine
and low paid jobs, as clerks, bookkeepers, typists, and secretaries,
in the business houses. Each treaty port had its cohort of foreign
drifters, stranded sailors, and pitiful failures. The bottom of the
foreign social pyramid and the underworld of vice and crime, rarely
noticed in the glowing reminiscences of treaty port life because, like
the Chinese in the concessions and settlements, they lacked real
power, were parts of the foreign establishment too.

Foreign "leaseholds," five in number, were territories ceded
by China during 1898 in the scramble for influence and strategic
bases following the opportune murder of two German missionaries
in Shantung in November 1897 which gave a pretext for the German
government to realize its long-standing desire to obtain a territorial
foothold in China. Kiaochow Bay in Shantung and surrounding territory, a total of 552 square kilometers, were leased to Germany for
ninety-nine years in March 1898, and concessions were given to
build three railroad lines in Shantung and to operate mines within
ten miles on either side of the roadbeds. Kiaochow was captured
by Japan in November 1914 after heavy fighting in which the Japanese suffered casualties of 616 killed and 1,228 wounded, a side-
show to World War I, and was returned to China only in 1922. The
Russians followed the Germans immediately with demands for a
twenty-five-year lease of the Liaotung peninsula (including the harbors of Port Arthur and Talienwan [Dairen] in southern Manchuria)

which was also granted in March. The Russian-controlled Chinese Eastern Railway Company was, in addition, given permission to build a branch line from Harbin to Port Arthur and Talienwan, the South Manchurian Railway, and to exploit timber and mines within the railroad zone. As a consequence of Russia's defeat by Japan, in 1905 the Liaotung leasehold and railroad rights were transferred to Japan. May 1898 saw the French extract a ninety-nine-year lease to the port of Kuangchou-wan, opposite Hainan Island in Kwangtung, as a naval station. In June, Britain obtained from China the lease for ninety-nine years of a northern extension to its Hong Kong colony, the "New Territories." Completing this series of raids on Chinese territory came the lease of Weihaiwei, a port in Shantung, to Great Britain in July 1898 "for as long a period as Port Arthur shall remain in the occupation of Russia."[4] The gratuitous rationale, contemporary and retrospective, offered for these aggressions was the necessity to maintain the international balance of power in East Asia.

In the leaseholds, in contrast to the concessions and settlements, China's sovereignty was explicitly extinguished for the terms of the several leases, as evidenced by the consensus among the treaty powers that their rights to extraterritorial consular jurisdiction which held in all other "Chinese" territory did not extend into these areas. And two of them, in Shantung and Manchuria, were at the core of the more extensive "spheres of influence" asserted by Germany, Russia, and Japan--together with Britain and France whose "spheres" were grounded on more diffuse claims--within Chinese territory.

The de facto basis for any power's claim to preferential or exclusive rights to make loans, construct and operate railroads, open mines, have its nationals employed as "advisers," or exercise some form of territorial jurisdiction in particular parts of China was the same tainted one, China's weakness and the threat of alien force, which sustained the derogations of sovereignty described in the previous paragraphs. Formally the several spheres of influence were based upon Chinese agreements with specified powers not to alienate certain areas to any third power; conventions or treaties to which China was a party but was in no position to reject; assertions by certain powers of rights due to contiguity; agreements among the powers to recognize each other's claims to which China was not a party; and claims to further rights arising from the fait accompli of predominant financial and commercial interests.

Russian rights in Manchuria derived from the secret treaty of alliance of May 1896, the construction of the Chinese Eastern Railway and its South Manchurian branch, and the lease of the Liaotung peninsula. From these bases, the Russian government proceeded to establish de facto political and military control within the railway zone, and strengthened its position through the occupation of Manchuria by Russian troops consequent to the Boxer uprising. Russian troops in Manchuria and increasing efforts to exert influence in Korea led to war with Japan in 1904-1905 and an embarrassing defeat for Russia. The lease of the Liaotung peninsula was transferred to Japan, as well as the South Manchurian Railway between Ch'angch'un and Port Arthur together with Russian "rights, privileges and properties" in the railway zone. After 1905, Russia continued to exercise effective political jurisdiction within the zone of the Chinese Eastern Railway and in cities and towns (Harbin, for example) in north Manchuria on that line, resulting in a division of spheres of influence in Manchuria with Japan which was formalized by Russo-Japanese conventions signed in 1907 and 1910. In 1914, the treaty powers except for the United States recognized Russian control over their nationals within the railway zone.[5]

By virtue of a nonalienation declaration made by China in 1898, Japan claimed the province of Fukien as a sphere of influence, but this was of little practical consequence. It was in south Manchuria, of course, that Japan's special status was progressively developed. China had no option but to give its consent to the assignment of Liaotung and of Russian railroad and mining rights in south Manchuria to Japan (Sino-Japanese treaty of December 1905), and by additional agreements to grant Japan "settlements" at Yingkow, Antung, and Mukden as well as further railroad concessions. The government-general of Kwantung was formally established in September 1906 to administer the leased territory (218 square miles) and the railway zones (108 square miles). Japan's sphere in Manchuria was implicitly acknowledged by France in 1907 (accompanied by a reciprocal Japanese recognition of the French sphere), by the United States in the Root-Takahira agreement of 1908, and by Russia as indicated above. And by Group II of the "Twenty-one Demands," which Japan forced the Yuan Shih-k'ai government to accept in 1915, the Japanese position in Manchuria was further consolidated: the Liaotung lease and the South Manchurian Railway concessions were extended to ninety-nine years; all of south Manchuria was opened to Japanese nationals for residence, commerce, and manufacture;

additional mining areas were made available to Japanese nationals; and commitments were made to give preference in the future to Japanese capitalists for loans and to Japanese nationals in the employment of political, military, and police advisers in south Manchuria and eastern Inner Mongolia.

The Kwantung leased territory became an island of Japanese society and culture on the Chinese mainland. Japanese language publications, colorful kimono, Shinto festivals, and yen notes as the official currency became part of the life of the colony and its principal city Dairen. From Kwantung northward through the economic heart of south Manchuria, the trunk line of the South Manchurian Railway ran 483 miles to Ch'ang-ch'un. It was served by feeder lines to the port of Yingkow, from Mukden (Shenyang) to Antung on the Korean border, and between Dairen and Port Arthur. In cities along the S.M.R. line and in the railroad zones on either side of the tracks, Japan exercised de facto political jurisdiction in spite of Chinese protests. The Kwantung government-general was practically coterminous with the South Manchurian Railway Company, the majority of whose shares were held by the Japanese government and which was placed under the supervision of the governor-general of Kwantung. The appointment of Japanese consuls in Manchuria was influenced by the S.M.R. Company and many served simultaneously as secretaries of the government-general. In addition to the various railroad lines, the S.M.R. Company operated coal mines at Fushun (near Mukden) and Yentai (near Liaoyang), steamer lines, and warehouses, and maintained schools, hospitals, experimental farms, public utilities, and "railway guards" within the railroad zones.

Before 1931, however, Japanese political authority in Manchuria was restricted to the leased territory and the railroad zones. Because of their favored economic position which funneled goods on the S.M.R. from the key market centers of Fengtien province to Dairen and Port Arthur, from where they were carried by Japanese steamer to Tientsin, Shanghai, Yokohama, and Osaka, the Japanese tended to overestimate their influence over Chang Tso-lin, the warlord ruler of Manchuria. The authority of the Peking government was small in Chang's satrapy, but he was equally skillful and effective in limiting the Japanese, ignoring them or conciliating them as the case may be, but successfully playing off competing Japanese interests against each other so as to maintain an authentically Chinese semi-independent regime.[6]

From November 1914 until the restoration of Shantung to China by the Sino-Japanese Shantung Agreement of February 1922 concluded in connection with the Washington Conference, Japan occupied the former German Kiaochow leasehold. The Japanese, in the face of strong Chinese protests, moved to control the Shantung railroads and mines with the object presumably of linking the railroads with those of Manchuria and thereby dominating north China. Between 1897 and 1914 Germany administered its leasehold as a colony under the jurisdiction of the Ministry of the Navy and attempted to use its railroad and mining concessions to extend its influence throughout the province of Shantung. Tsingtao, with a population of 55,000 Chinese and 5,000 Europeans and Japanese in 1913 (the total population of the Kiaochow leasehold was about 200,000), was known to foreigners as the "Brighton of the Far East." Its climate and the marvelous east beach of the outer bay (Auguste Viktoria Bay), more than a mile in length on the Yellow Sea, made it a fashionable summer resort. The Strand Hotel accommodated five hundred guests and together with the racecourse was situated near the beach. On the southern slope down to the bay there grew up the "European town" of Tsingtao with its symmetrical plan, paved and illuminated (first by gaslight and then electricity) streets lined with sidewalks and large trees, and the villas and gardens of the wealthy German inhabitants. Chinese servants lived in "coolie houses" in the rear of the main buildings. The bulk of the Chinese population resided in the "Chinese town" which had been physically separated from the European sector by the demolition and removal of inconveniently proximate Chinese villages. Tsingtao was developed into a first-class port, and the municipality operated modern water and sewage systems, efficient hospitals, a German grammar school, and a German-Chinese high school founded in 1909 as a joint effort by the German government and Chinese officials. Industrial investment in the city itself was relatively small, the most famous enterprise being the Anglo-German Brewery Company established in 1904, which produced the still renowned Tsingtao beer.

The Schantung Eisenbahn Gesellschaft and the Schantung Bergbau Gesellschaft, both formed in 1899 by a syndicate consisting of the financial houses which organized the Deutsch-Asiatische Bank in Shanghai together with German firms (e.g., Carlowitz and Company) in China, were in theory Sino-German companies. In practice the capital and management of the railroad built from Tsingtao to Tsinanfu were entirely German, as was also the case for the coal mines opened at Wei-hsien and Hung-shan. The German banking syndicate and British financial interests, both with the backing of their governments, agreed in 1898 in connection with plans to build a railroad from Tientsin to the Yangtze River that the German sphere of influence would extend northward into Hopei province while predominant British influence in the Yangtze valley and in Shansi province was recognized in return. Even in Shantung, however, the Germans found it increasingly difficult to realize the preferential treatment which they claimed. A combination of German diplomatic isolation after 1900, fear of jeopardizing commercial interests elsewhere in China by exclusive claims in Shantung, and a concerted Chinese effort to limit the German sphere in Shantung effectively confined the Germans to their leasehold and to a narrow interpretation of the railroad and mining concessions. Unlike Manchuria, Chinese and not German railroad guards provided protection in the Tsingtao-Tsinan railroad zone; efforts to take over the postal and telegraph services along the railroad failed; only part of the mining concessions could be exploited; and even Tsingtao's status as a free port was ended in 1906. [7]

By virtue of their contiguity to the French colony of Vietnam, France claimed a sphere of influence in the southern Chinese provinces of Yunnan, Kweichow, and Kwangsi. France was given a concession for a railroad from Vietnam across the border into Yunnan in 1898 (construction began in 1903, entirely French financed and managed), obtained assurances that none of the provinces bordering Vietnam would be alienated to a third power, and secured a leasehold of Kwangchou-wan as noted earlier. French commerce, especially in Yunnan, received preferential treatment by virtue of French ownership of the railroad, but few other concessions were obtained or exploited, and no local political control comparable to that of Russia and Japan in Manchuria was realized.

Britain, until World War I, dominated foreign commerce in China, was China's leading foreign creditor, held major railroad and mining concessions, provided the majority of the foreign personnel in the Maritime Customs Service and the Salt Administration, and accounted for half of the Protestant missionaries. In a sense, its sphere of influence extended throughout the territory of China, and it would have preferred to keep things as they were before the international rivalries of the last part of the nineteenth century extended their shadows to China in anticipation, as some saw it, of a carving up of the "Chinese melon." The British response to the scramble for concessions which followed the Sino-Japanese war of 1894-1895 was at least a partial abandonment of the commitment to equal and open commercial activity in China (the "open door") upon which British predominance had hitherto been based, and its replacement by compensatory concessions from China and agreements with the rival powers which tacitly accepted but also sought to limit their spheres of influence.[8] Apart from its Hong Kong colony, the New Territories leased in 1898, and Weihaiwei which was never developed as a strategic naval base, the British sphere lacked the specific territorial underpinnings and thus the temptation to develop a local political role comparable to the Japanese in Manchuria. What was obtained from the Chinese government in February 1898 was a promise that the Yangtze valley provinces would never be alienated to a third power and the implicit recognition of Britain's claim to special consideration in the granting of railroad and mining concessions in this region. While the Ch'ing court was in no position to resist foreign demands frontally, it was not completely impotent. Thus, in spite of these vague promises to Britain, the concession for the Peking-Hankow trunkline was granted to a Belgian syndicate (the majority of whose shares were held by the French Compagnie des Chemins de fer Chinois). The British government reacted with strong support in Peking for the British and Chinese Corporation (formed by the Hong Kong and Shanghai Banking Corporation and Jardine, Matheson and Company) which resulted in railroad concessions in the Yangtze valley (the Tientsin-Chinkiang line from the Shantung border southward, and the Shanghai-Nanking and Soochow-Hangchow-Ningpo lines), between Canton and Kowloon, and in Manchuria (the line from Shanhaikuan to Newchwang), all granted in 1898. Simultaneously the Peking Syndicate, another British group backed by the financiers Carl Meyer and Lord Rothschild, obtained concessions to develop mines in Shansi and Honan, and for the construction of an east-west railroad (Taokow-Chinghua line) connecting its mines in Honan to the Peking-Hankow main line. Political as much as financial reasons--that is, the broad political goal of preventing the consolidation of rival spheres of influence--underlay this British concession hunting. But direct control in the concession areas was neither envisaged nor achieved.

The substantial reshaping of the international system by World War I, together with profound changes in China's domestic political situation, greatly reduced the significance of the foreign spheres of influence carved out at the turn of the century--except, a major exception, for the Japanese in Manchuria. While the continued existence of some foreign railroad and mining rights, in various formats, did not make Chinese nationalism happy, by 1920 these were relatively minor facets of the foreign presence in China.

No more than a rough estimate of the number of foreign nationals resident in China is possible. How many tens of thousands of Koreans, for example, had moved across the Yalu River into Manchuria? The Maritime Customs Service annually compiled estimates of the number of foreign "firms" and residents at the open ports, which probably covered the majority of the places where there were any substantial concentrations of aliens other than the Koreans in Manchuria. Dairen, for example, in the Kwantung leased territory, was included, as was Harbin, from 1910, but not Tsingtao in the Kiaochow leasehold while it was under German control. Table 1 shows the customs estimates for 1903, 1906, 1909, 1911, 1913, 1916, 1918, and 1921.[9] The figures in the table are defective in several respects. Before 1910 the bulk of the Russian population in Manchuria, which was heavily concentrated in Harbin, was not included; the sudden increase of Russian nationals from 1909 to 1911 is only an apparent one. (Also not yet reflected is the influx from Siberia after 1920 of stateless "White Russian" refugees without extraterritorial rights who eventually numbered more than 200,000.) Similarly, the largely German foreign population of Tsingtao, which was 4,084 of whom 2,275 were military and officials in 1910, was excluded. Not all of the missionaries resident in the interior were covered in the Customs estimates, and foreign troops stationed in China were completely omitted.

Fairly accurately reflected is the fact of the large influx of Japanese into Manchuria after 1905, although the totals are too low. The Japanese government reported, for example, that 121,956 of its nationals were resident in China in 1914. After the capture of Kiaochow in 1914 and the movement of Japanese into Shantung, the main centers of Japanese residence were Dairen, Tsingtao, Shanghai, Antung, and Amoy in that order. Nearly 40 percent of the combined British, American, French, and German populations were located in Shanghai. Note the relatively large increase in the total number of American residents after World War I, and the decrease in the German figures. Excluding Dairen and Harbin in Manchuria, the cities in China proper with the largest number of foreign resi-

TABLE 1

ESTIMATED NUMBER OF FOREIGN "FIRMS" AND RESIDENTS IN CHINA*

	British		U.S.		French		German		Russian		Japanese		Total**	
	Firms	Res	Firms	Res	Firms	Res	Firms	Res	Firms	Res	Firms	Res	Firms	Res
1903	420	5,662	114	2,542	71	1,213	159	1,658	24	361	361	5,287	1,292	20,404
1906	492	9,256	112	3,447	94	2,189	199	1,939	20	273	739	15,548	1,837	38,597
1909	502	9,499	113	3,168	84	1,818	232	2,341	83	336	1,492	55,401	2,801	88,310
1911	606	10,256	111	3,470	112	1,925	258	2,758	313	51,221	1,283	78,306	2,863	153,522
1913	590	8,966	131	5,340	106	2,292	296	2,949	1,229	56,765	1,269	80,219	3,805	113,827
1916	644	9,099	187	5,580	116	2,374	281	3,792	1,422	55,235	1,858	104,275	4,724	185,613
1918	606	7,953	234	5,766	156	2,580	75	2,651	1,154	59,719	4,483	159,950	6,930	244,527
1921	703	9,298	412	8,230	222	2,453	92	1,255	1,613	68,250	6,141	144,434	9,511	240,769

*Defects of the table are discussed in the text.
**Including other nationalities not separately listed.

dents were, in descending order with estimates for 1911 in paren-
theses, Shanghai (30,292), Tientsin (6,334), Hankow (2,862), Amoy
(1,931), and Canton (1,324). Japanese nationals in Shanghai (17,682)
formed the largest foreign contingent, followed by British (5,270),
Portuguese (3,000), Americans (1,350), Germans (1,100), French
(705), and Russians (275).

Apart from Japanese and Russian civilians in Manchuria, the
size of some of the major categories of foreigners in China in the
second decade of the twentieth century may be estimated as follows:
foreign employees of the Chinese central and local governments,
2,000 (including 1,300 in the Customs Service); diplomatic personnel,
500 (led in numbers by Japan, Great Britain, and the United States);
missionaries, 9,100 (6,600 Protestants and 2,500 Catholics); military detachments and police, 26,000 (including 17,000 Japanese
troops and 2,000 police in Manchuria); and businessmen in the thousands, the number being impossible to estimate, but--except for
the Japanese who were also engaged in more menial occupations--
constituting most of the foreign residents of Shanghai and of the
other major treaty ports.[10]

The Customs data on foreign firms are especially misleading.
It appears that the definition used was a highly elastic one, so that
for Manchuria even the smallest shop serving the Russian and Japanese populations was included, while in China proper both the Shanghai head office and the branches of the same firm in other ports
were separately enumerated. Of the 643 foreign firms in Shanghai
in 1911, 40 percent (258) were British, 16 percent (103) German,
9 percent (59) American, and 7 percent (47) Japanese, with the
remainder scattered. After Shanghai, the cities in China proper
with the largest number of foreign establishments in 1911 were
Tientsin (260), Amoy (240), Hankow (125), and Canton (102).

What these foreign nationals and firms of the several treaty
powers--and missionaries stationed in the interior who will be discussed below--enjoyed in common were the rights and privileges of
the extraterritorial system. Beginning with the basic concession of
"consular jurisdiction" in the 1842-1844 treaties, by the accumulation
of formal agreements forced upon China or by unilateral assertions
of privilege, the entire "foreign establishment" which is described in
this essay was essentially exempted from the jurisdiction of the Chinese polity. All disputes in which the plaintiffs were Chinese,

whether private individuals or agencies of the Chinese government, and the defendants nationals of treaty powers were adjudicated in the courts of the powers concerned and according to the laws of those powers. This was true for both criminal and civil cases. Controversies between nationals of the same treaty power, or between nationals of different powers, were likewise removed from Chinese purview. Extraterritorial jurisdiction was exercised primarily by consular officials in the ports and by diplomatic officials in Peking upon appeal. Both Great Britain and the United States, in addition, maintained national courts which sat in Shanghai, the British Supreme Court in China established in 1904, and the United States Court for China established in 1906.

It was unquestionably offensive to Chinese nationalism that foreign criminal offenders on the whole received easier treatment in the consular courts than they would have enjoyed in their home countries. The much greater derogation of sovereignty, with larger consequences for China's economy and society, however, was the inability of Chinese authorities to restrict, regulate, license, or tax directly foreign individuals or firms of the treaty powers who as "legal persons" were subject only to the laws of their own consular courts. As a foreigner carried his extraterritorial rights with him wherever he went for business or pleasure, this freedom from effective regulation operated not merely in the treaty ports but everywhere. Foreign banks enjoyed extraterritorial rights; their issuance of currency could not be controlled, nor did they accept any other regulation. Individuals and corporations were immune from direct Chinese taxation not by any specific treaty right, but because tax officials accepted the futility of attempting enforcement through foreign courts which applied only the laws of their particular countries--none of which, of course, included Chinese tax legislation. Missionaries and other foreigners freely established schools which enjoyed extraterritoriality and thus were not subject to regulation as to plant, curriculum, or teachers' qualifications. Behind the screen of extraterritoriality, an assertive foreign press subjected China and the Chinese to its frequently carping and malicious criticism without encumbrance. It was, moreover, a common abuse that foreign citizens or subjects of nontreaty powers were claimed as their own nationals by the powers that did have treaty rights, and thus also removed from the jurisdiction of the Chinese courts. "The treaties," one American diplomat summarized, "had come to be interpreted . . . as providing protection to Americans, and other foreigners enjoying extraterritorial rights and privileges, from interference of any sort or degree in their activities by the authorities or agents of the Chinese government. The basic original right of freedom from Chinese court jurisdiction had been extended and broadened to include freedom from Chinese administrative control except in matters explicitly provided for in the treaties."[11]

In the mixed courts of the foreign settlements at Shanghai, Amoy, and Hankow the arm of extraterritoriality extended even into controversies in which the parties concerned were formally subject to Chinese law and procedure. The Mixed Court of the Shanghai International Settlement was established by agreement with the Shanghai taotai in 1864 to try Chinese offenders within the Settlement, civil claims by foreigners against Chinese, and claims by foreigners or Chinese against foreigners without consular representation, all matters within Chinese jurisdiction according to the treaties. A Chinese magistrate was delegated by the taotai to preside over the Court. In those cases in which their nationals were plaintiffs, the treaty powers had the right (stated in Article XVII of the Treaty of Tientsin) to be represented by foreign "assessors" who, together with the Chinese judges, would "examine into the merits of the case, and decide it equitably." Even before the Mixed Court was taken over in 1911 by the authorities of the International Settlement, the power of the Chinese magistrate had been much reduced while the influence of the foreign assessors, except in purely Chinese civil cases, had in practice become predominant. A test case in 1883 ended the magistrate's right to arrest Chinese residents of the Settlement; in the famous Su-pao case of 1903 the Chinese right to extradite "political" offenders from the Settlement was restricted; and from 1905 the Settlement municipal police rather than Chinese "runners" executed the writs and warrants of the Mixed Court. In the course of the 1911 Revolution, the Shanghai Municipal Council assumed control of the appointment and payment of the Chinese magistrates of the Court; and the foreign assessors now also formally heard Chinese civil cases. This supposedly temporary measure, having no legal justification whatever and based entirely upon alleged foreign dissatisfaction with Chinese judicial practices, was ended only with the "rendition" of the Mixed Court to Chinese control in 1926.

Their extraterritorial rights were of course lost by German and Austro-Hungarian nationals when China entered World War I on

the Allied side in August 1917. Similarly, the October Revolution
brought to an end the formal privileges of the Russians, through
the closing of the moribund Tsarist consulates and the Russian concessions in Hankow and Tientsin by the Chinese government in September 1920, and by the voluntary renunciation of extraterritoriality
(although not of its control of the Chinese Eastern Railway) by the
Soviet government. Without force--that is, in the absence of the
military support or at least the acquiescence of the treaty powers
collectively--the extraterritorial system could not be maintained
even against a weak China.

Military force had brought the foreign establishment in China
into existence, and its continuous deployment on Chinese soil and
in riverine and coastal waters constituted in symbol, and sometimes
in practice, the effective sanction behind the formally correct diplomatic measures which were constantly exerted to maintain the treaty
rights of the foreigners and to assure the protection of their persons
and property. The basis for the presence of gunboats on the rivers
and in the treaty ports and of larger naval vessels along China's
coast was a very liberal interpretation of Article LII of the 1858
Treaty of Tientsin which stated that "British ships of war coming
for no hostile purpose, or being engaged in the pursuit of pirates,
shall be at liberty to visit all ports within the dominions of the
Empire of China." In 1896, British naval tonnage on the China
station totaled 59,000; Russia nearly the same; France 28,000; Germany 23,000; and the United States 18,000 tons. "H.B.M. Squadron,"
now up to a total of 70,000 tons, numbered thirty-three vessels in
1908, of which four were armored cruisers, two second-class cruisers, and the remaining twenty-seven smaller vessels including river
gunboats.

The use or threat of foreign gunboats was a common occurrence
in the "missionary incidents" which punctuated the last half of the
nineteenth century. Chungking was reached by British gunboats for
the first time in 1900. French naval vessels carried out pioneer
surveys of the upper Yangtze in the early 1900s seeking to discover
routes for the extension of trade from their railroad into Yunnan.
The Germans were active around Poyang Lake, much to the anxiety
of the British who considered the Yangtze valley as their special
preserve. At the end of the nineteenth century, as noted above,
strategic naval bases in addition to Hong Kong--Tsingtao, Port Arthur,
Kwangchou-wan, Weihaiwei--were ceded as leaseholds to the several
powers and brought cruisers and battleships on a regular basis to
Chinese waters.

Before 1903, the United States did not maintain a fleet of gunboats regularly stationed at key points on the Yangtze in the British manner. Occasional vessels from the Asiatic fleet perhaps once a year steamed their way up and down that waterway. The American Yangtze Patrol--formally the Second Division, Third Squadron, Pacific Fleet from 1908 to 1919--numbered six to eight quite antiquated gunboats at the time of World War I, as compared to fifteen modern gunboats operated by the British. Patrols in the early republic were largely routine and most of the excitement for the sailors was on shore. But the vessels were there "to keep peace on the river" and to leave no question about the willingness of the treaty powers to protect their rights.

Foreign troops and police guards were a more conspicuous part of the foreign establishment in China in the early twentieth century than they had been in the last decades of the nineteenth. Apart from the expeditionary forces which defeated China in 1840-1842, 1858-1860, and 1894-1895 and were then withdrawn, foreign ground forces were limited to the municipal police which grew up in the several settlements and concessions and the international militias ("volunteer corps") at these same places. The Shanghai Volunteer Corps, the largest, in 1913 numbered fifty-nine officers (mainly British) and about one thousand rank and file (half British, the rest scattered among fifteen nationalities). Britain's military units in its Hong Kong colony may perhaps be counted as another exception. The leaseholds seized from China in 1898 and then the Boxer Protocol imposed by the powers in 1901 brought into being a permanent and more sizable military presence.

By the terms of the Protocol the powers were permitted to maintain armed detachments in Peking ("Legation Guards"), to occupy key points along the railway from Peking to the sea, and to station troops in Tientsin from which city Chinese troops were to be excluded. In 1913, the Peking Legation Guards totalled 2,075 (370 British, 329 American, 307 Japanese, 301 Russian, 288 French, 199 Italian, 151 German, 64 Austrian, 35 Dutch, and 31 Belgian). By 1922 the number had been reduced to 997, the German, Austrian, and Russian contingents having disappeared as a consequence of the loss of extraterritorial rights by these powers, and the rest (except for the Americans who totalled 354) having decreased their forces somewhat. Foreign troops in Tientsin in 1913 numbered 6,219 (2,218 British, 1,021 French, 975 American, 883 Japanese, 808 Russian, 282 German, 21 Austrian, and 11 Italian). The 1922 total was 2,720 (982 French, 762 Japanese, 504 American, and 472 British). Elsewhere in north China, principally along the railroad from Peking to Shanhaikuan there were 1,253 foreign troops in 1913, and 601 in 1922.

The British and French garrisons at Weihaiwei and Kuangchou-wan were miniscule, but German military and naval detachments in Tsingtao totalled 2,300. Four battalions of Japanese troops, 2,100 officers and men, replaced the Germans in Shantung in 1914, where they were stationed along the Tsingtao-Tsinanfu railroad until 1922. They were supported by a substantial force of gendarmerie. The fighting at Hankow in 1911 led to the dispatch of British, German, Russian, and Japanese troops to that port to protect their respective nationals. All but the Japanese were withdrawn in 1912; a Japanese batallion of five hundred men together with detachments of special troops remained in Hankow until 1922. In south Manchuria, with headquarters in Liaoyang in the leased territory, Japan normally stationed a full infantry division with supporting cavalry and artillery. Sixteen batallions of railway guards totalling ten thousand troops were in place along the Chinese Eastern Railway and in the South Manchurian Railway zones in 1920. The presence of these railway guards was justified by provisions in the 1905 Portsmouth Peace Treaty between Japan and Russia, which the Chinese asserted they had not assented to in their agreement with Japan of December 1905 recognizing the transfer of Liaotung and the South Manchurian Railway from Russia to Japan. Japanese police in Manchuria in 1920 numbered 811 in the leased territory and 1,052 more in the South Manchurian and Antung-Mukden railway zones.[12]

Like the gunboats on the Yangtze, even the total number of these foreign troops and police was perhaps not a very formidable military force. Where their presence had some legal basis in China's forced consent to an international agreement such as the Boxer Protocol, they nevertheless were blatant infringements of China's sovereignty. This was even more unmistakable in the case of the railroad zones in Manchuria and Shantung which the Japanese occupied over repeated Chinese protests. More important than the formal legal basis of this foreign military occupation, which perhaps was arguable, is the understanding of what the stationing of foreign troops on Chinese soil implied--the ability and willingness of the extraterritorial powers to employ force if necessary in support of what they unilaterally considered their acquired rights.

II. MINISTERS AND CONSULS

The Diplomatic Body in Peking met in the house
of the doyen, that is to say in the British or, if Sir
John was away, in the Spanish legation.

When we met in the British legation in warm
weather, the windows would be open on to a small
inner courtyard, where the lilac blossomed in the
spring. The legation parrot used to sit out there
and join in our discussions (sometimes very aptly)
with a hoarse guffaw, or a subdued chuckle, or a
sudden screech. He was a talking parrot, but he
only spoke Chinese, so that his remarks were un-
intelligible to most of the assembled diplomats.[1]

In the first years of the republic the most conspicuous component of the foreign establishment in China, the Diplomatic Body in
Peking, consisted of envoys extraordinary and ministers plenipotentiary from fifteen countries, in the order in which treaty relations
were established: Great Britain, the United States, France, Belgium,
Sweden, Russia, Germany, Portugal, Denmark, the Netherlands, Spain
Italy, Austria-Hungary, and Brazil. Peru, Norway (separated from
Sweden in 1905), and Mexico also had treaty relations with China,
making eighteen nations in all who participated in the benefits of the
"most-favored-nation" clause, but in 1913 did not have representatives resident in Peking. Within the diplomatic body, the eleven
signers of the Boxer Protocol of 1901--Germany, Austria-Hungary,
Belgium, Spain, the United States, France, Great Britain, Italy,
Japan, the Netherlands, and Russia--formed a closer circle, and
even more select were the powers which exerted real influence in
China as in the world: Great Britain, Japan, Russia, the United
States, Germany, and France.

Signor Vare, the Italian minister during World War I, is approximately correct about the linguistic accomplishments, so far as Chinese is concerned, of his colleagues. Except for Sir John Newell
Jordan, G.C.I.E., K.C.B., K.C.M.G., who had first come to China
as a student interpreter in 1876 and had served long and well in the
British consular service in China and as Minister to Korea before
his appointment in 1906 as H.M. Envoy Extraordinary and Minister
Plenipotentiary in Peking, the foreign ministers were typically pro-

25

fessional "diplomats" who moved from posting to posting (for example, as of 1913, Baron E. de Cartier de Marchienne of Belgium, Count P. Ahlefeldt-Laurvig of Denmark, Count Carlo Sforza of Italy, or M. Alexandre Conty of France). Of Jordan, who continued as minister until 1920, one of his Peking colleagues wrote: "To him, China was not one post among many. It represented the beginning and the end of his career and apologia pro vita sua. . . . I do not profess to know what passed in Sir John's mind, but it seemed to me that his world consisted of the British Empire and China, with Russia and Japan looming in the background (sometimes inconveniently near) and a lot of other powers fussing round and interfering in matters which did not really concern them and which they imperfectly understood."2 Sir Ernest Mason Satow, Jordan's predecessor in Peking from 1900 to 1906, while more of a diplomatic professional than Sir John (he was the author of the much acclaimed A Guide to Diplomatic Practice, 1917 and later editions), also began his career as a student interpreter, and reputedly spoke some Chinese as well as excellent Japanese. Satow had spent long years in the consular service in Japan, Siam, Peru, and Morocco before being appointed minister to Tokyo in 1895. Sir Ernest was described by his private secretary as "an austere man. He was very hard on his staff and exacted a tremendous amount of work from them, but, as he used to say, he had been brought up in a hard school--the school of Sir Harry Parkes. . . . I learnt from Sir Ernest to follow Lord Elgin's maxim for dealing with Chinese officials. Never make a demand which is not absolutely just; when you make a just demand see that you get it."3 The British were represented in Peking in the first part of the twentieth century, in other words, by diplomats of a sort who matched Britain's still dominant place in China's foreign relations and international commerce.

The Japanese, however, since the war of 1894-95, had been catching up fast in both respects. There was much coming and going at the Japanese legation in Peking in the first two decades of the twentieth century, with affairs frequently in the hands of a chargé, but overall the Japanese ministers were professional diplomats (graduates of the Law Faculty of Tokyo Imperial University) who had had considerable prior experience in consular posts in China and probably therefore had some knowledge of the Chinese language. Uchida Yasuya, minister 1901-1906, had been charge in 1896 while first secretary of the legation. He later filled other major ambassadorial posts, and in 1911, 1918-1923, and 1932 served as foreign minister,

on the last occasion concurrently with the presidency of the South
Manchurian Railway Company. His successor during 1906-1908, and
again in 1916-1918, was Hayashi Gonsuke, educated in England as
well as Tokyo, who at other times was ambassador to Great Britain
and Russia, and briefly foreign minister. Ijuin Hikokichi, minister
1908-1913, first came to China in 1893 as consul at Chefoo. During
1901-1907 he was consul-general at Tientsin. He was later governor
of the Kwantung Leased Territory, and foreign minister briefly in
1923. Yamaza Enjiro had been secretary of the Japanese legation
in Seoul prior to his brief tenure as minister in Peking in 1913-1914.
Hioki Eki, who transmitted Japan's "Twenty-one Demands" in 1915,
had served in Korea during 1894-1899, then in Peking as first secretary and chargé in 1900-1902, before his appointment as minister in
1914. After several tours in Europe, he returned to China as Japan's
representative at the 1925 Tariff Conference. His long service in
Tientsin, Peking, and elsewhere as consul and chargé (in 1914, 1915,
1916), culminated in the appointment of Obata Torikichi as minister
during the years 1918-1923. The Japanese, together with the British,
as their diplomatic documents reveal, in these years had the closest
knowledge of any of the foreign powers of Chinese political and economic affairs--a product not only of the caliber (and size) of their
Peking missions but also of their consular services and the multiple
informal sources of information open to them as a consequence of
their commanding presence in China.

Former Republican Congressman Edwin Hurd Conger, the American minister 1898-1905, reached that office through his friendship
with President McKinley. His successor during 1905-1909, William
Woodville Rockhill, however, was a professional diplomat, who in
the 1880s had been posted to Peking and Seoul, as well as a considerable linguist and scholar (of Tibetan Buddhism, Central Asia, and
China's premodern relations with the Western world, Korea, and
Southeast Asia). William James Calhoun, in Peking 1909-1913, long
active in the Republican party in Illinois and with some experience
as a special envoy for Presidents McKinley and Roosevelt in Cuba
and Venezuela, was President Taft's choice for the Peking post.
Paul Samuel Reinsch, minister during 1913-1919, was again a political appointee, this time of President Wilson who was impressed by
Reinsch's scholarly anti-imperialist writings (e. g., World Politics
at the End of the Nineteenth Century, 1900; Colonial Government,
1902; Colonial Administration, 1905; and Intellectual and Political
Currents in the Far East, 1911) as Professor of Political Science
at the University of Wisconsin. Reinsch's memoirs, An American

Diplomat in China (1922) reveal a considerable if ineffectual sympathy
with Chinese aspirations for greater international equality. Shortly
after Shantung was awarded to Japan by the Versailles Conference,
Reinsch resigned his post.

Much of the actual day to day contact with the Chinese Foreign
Ministry and other officials in Peking, limited as it was, was handled
by the "Chinese secretaries" of the principal legations, who in consequence frequently influenced the outlook of their mission chiefs.
Sidney Barton, for example, was a dominant figure in the British
legation as its Chinese secretary during 1911-1922. Barton had
entered the consular service as student interpreter in 1895 and risen
through the ranks. As perhaps might be anticipated from the hus-
band of the eldest daughter of a director of Jardine, Matheson and
Company, he was a vigorous and at times insensitive defender of
British interests, inclined to forceful measures which endeared him
to the British community in China but made him distinctly disliked
by the Chinese with whom he had to deal. In 1922 he was appointed
consul-general at Shanghai and served in that post until 1929 when
he was promoted to the diplomatic rank of British minister in Addis
Ababa.

The United States legation tended to select its Chinese secretaries from American missionaries in China. Edward T. Williams,
Chinese secretary 1901-1908, served under the Foreign Christian
Missionary Society from 1887 until 1896 when he left the ministry
to accept an appointment as translator at the American Consulate-
General in Shanghai. He was first secretary of the American legation in Peking 1911-1913, and served several months as chargé,
between the departure of Calhoun and the arrival of Reinsch--a
period which included the American recognition of the Republic of
China and the "Second Revolution." During 1914-1918 he was chief
of the Far Eastern Division of the Department of State. Williams
left government service in 1918 to become Agassiz Professor of
Oriental Languages and Literature at the University of California at
Berkeley where his scholarly contributions were modest. Succeeding
Williams was Charles D. Tenney who had come to China in 1882
under the auspices of the American Board of Commissioners for
Foreign Missions. Tenney retired from missionary work in 1886
and spent the next two decades in Tientsin where he was engaged
in educational activities blessed by the successive Governors-general
Li Hung-chang and Yuan Shih-k'ai. He served as principal of the

Anglo-Chinese School from 1886 to 1895, and in 1895 was selected
to head the newly established government university at Tientsin
(after 1900 known as Peiyang University). From 1902 to 1906, when
he left the presidency of Peiyang, he was also superintendent of high
and middle schools in Chihli. Except for a brief interval Tenney
held the post of Chinese secretary to the American legation from
1908 until 1919, and served as chargé with the rank of first secretary in 1919-1920. Being widely acquainted with Chinese officialdom,
including President Yuan Shih-k'ai, Tenney's role in the legation was
presumably an influential one. Willys R. Peck, assistant Chinese
secretary 1908-1913, Chinese secretary 1913-1914 and 1919-1926,
had been born in Tientsin to missionary parents. He was appointed
a student interpreter in 1906 after graduation from the University of
California, and between 1914 and 1919 held consular posts at Tsingtao, Hankow, and Tientsin. Peck remained a prominent figure in
the conduct of American relations with China until his retirement in
1945, serving as counselor of the embassy during 1935-1940.

The Legation Quarter in Peking where the ministers and their
staffs resided was an anomaly in international law, established by
Article VII of the Boxer Protocol of 1901 which stipulated: "The
Chinese Government has agreed that the quarter occupied by the
legations shall be considered as one specially reserved for their
use and placed under their exclusive control, in which Chinese shall
not have the right to reside and which may be made defensible. . . ."
Located just to the south of the Tartar City, protected by a fortified
outer wall (and permanent military guards within), and bounded on
the north by a "glacis"--an open space intended for polo, football,
exercising ponies, and drilling legation guards, which in fact was
the area formerly occupied by the imperial Hanlin Academy which
had been razed during the Boxer uprising--the new Legation Quarter
was some ten times larger than before 1900. Sir Ernest Satow,
among others, rebuked his colleagues in 1904 for their excessive
appetites.[4] In practice the Diplomatic Body extended its "rights"
considerably beyond the provisions of Article VII. Parts of the
glacis were leased to hotels, bars frequented by legation soldiers,
and a licensed brothel. Contrary to the theory that the glacis was
the joint property of them all, building permits were issued by individual powers, for a consideration of course. Within the Legation
Quarter itself were to be found commercial enterprises, shops, educational institutions, and a large number of nondiplomatic personnel--
although the Chinese had never intended to open Peking as another

center for foreign residence and trade. Among others, in the Quarter or its immediate neighborhood were the Hotel du Nord, the Hotel de Pekin, the Grand Hotel des Wagon-Lits (swarming with seekers after loan, railroad, and mining contracts); the Hongkong and Shanghai Bank, the Russo-Chinese Bank, the Deutsch-Asiatische Bank, and the Yokohama Specie Bank; several large foreign stores; a soldiers' YMCA: two Methodist Episcopal hospitals; a Catholic church for the legation guards; the Methodist Mission Church (with accommodations for 1,500 people), a Methodist girls' school, and "Peking University" (also Methodist); the London Mission's Lockhart Medical College; the church and school of the American Board of Commissioners for Foreign Missions; and the Mission for the Blind. While de jure the only Chinese permitted in the Quarter were the servants and employees of the legations in their special uniforms, in fact at times large numbers of Chinese lived in the Legation Quarter, frequently at the Wagon-Lits Hotel which was noted as a place of refuge for the "outs" in the Peking government after 1911. The "right of asylum" was claimed and enforced by the Diplomatic Body time and again: Chang Hsün, for example, hid in the Netherlands legation after the collapse of his brief coup in 1917.

Joint administration of the Legation Quarter was achieved only in 1914, replacing the three distinct sections (western, British, and eastern) which prior to that time had each had its own administration and regulations. An Administrative Commission composed of three representatives of the legations of the Boxer Protocol powers and two representatives of the residents of the Quarter oversaw the new General Police Regulations and Road Regulations. A land tax paid by the legations and private residents supported this minimal administration.

The situation probably improved after the republic came into being, and was somewhat better in the last decade of the Ch'ing dynasty than it had been before 1900, but it was still the case that for the most part the Peking diplomats lived a life apart from that of the Chinese. Charles Denby, American minister 1885-1898, recalled:

> Arriving at Peking, the first duty of the diplomatic stranger is to call on the Tsung-li-Yamen, foreign office, to pay his respects and be recognized in his official capacity. . . . The call on the Yamen is the only one

the stranger is required to make. In other countries
official calls are the dread of the visitor, but there
was in my day no court circle at Peking, and social
intercourse with the foreigners was frowned on by the
empress. . . . The absence of the necessity of meeting each other socially was a great relief both to the
Chinese and to the foreigners. Except on rare occasions, social intercourse would have been exceedingly
tedious for both parties.[5]

During the halcyon days of the post-Boxer Manchu reforms, younger
foreign-educated officials of the Foreign Ministry and the Ministry of
Communications were known to pass evenings at poker with staff members of the legations. But life in the Peking foreign community, diplomatic and private, was characteristically one of self-imposed isolation, of which the most dedicated exponents were probably the British
who "allayed their nostalgia with dinners and dancing, gossip and golf,
happily ignorant of the customs or language or feelings of the people
they lived among."[6] The Italian minister, thinking back to 1918,
described "a sort of diplomatic mountain fastness. For the women
and children, this was a good thing, if only from the point of view of
hygiene. But most of the diplomats were isolated from and out of
sympathy with the country they lived in."[7]

However self-contained, life in Peking was hardly one of physical deprivation for the diplomatic community. The British legation
compound in 1900

was an area covering just over three acres. The compound and dwelling had formerly been the residence of
Duke Liang and was rented by Her Majesty's Government. The Main Building was the Minister's residence,
a beautiful Chinese building with an imposing entrance
by a raised pathway passing under two stately porticos,
known in Chinese as t'ing'rh. All these were covered
with the official green tiles, permitted only to officials
of high rank, yellow being reserved for the Imperial
Palace. The Secretaries were housed in bungalows,
with the exception of the First Secretary who had a
foreign-style two-storied house. The students and
chancery assistants were located in three sets of buildings: the Escort Quarters, a two-storied building in

> Chinese style; the Stable Quarters, a two-storied for-
> eign building in the stables; and the Students' Quarters,
> a long two-storied building in foreign style. There
> was also the chapel, a theater and a bowling alley.[8]

Even the politically unimportant Italian legation, besides the minister's residence and that of the first secretary, included

> a house each for the first and second "Chinese secre-
> taries" (or interpreters) and for the legation chaplain.
> A chapel (as big as most churches) with a ceiling that
> had been sent out from Italy; stables for eighteen horses,
> with exercise ground and a large stable yard; a wash-
> house; a water tower; hothouses and two little buildings
> for the Chinese servants, the whole enclosed in a large
> shady garden. Besides all this, and connected with the
> legation compound, were barracks for the naval guard,
> with hospital, kitchens, houses for officers and petty
> officers; messrooms, offices, prison and munitions de-
> pot. Also a building for the apparatus to distil water,
> and more stables.[9]

The residence of the American minister was built in "stately colonial
renaissance style . . . of imported American materials, and a government architect was expressly sent to put up the legation buildings.
. . . At a distance from the 'compound,' or enclosure, which sur-
rounds the minister's residence, fronting on a central plaza, there
is a veritable hamlet of additional houses occupied by secretaries,
attaches, consular students, and the clerical staff. It is a pictur-
esque Chinese village, with an antique temple and many separate
houses, each with its garden enclosed within high walls--a rescued
bit of ancient China in the midst of the European monotony of the
Legation Quarter."[10] The first secretary of the Italian legation in
1913 noted that he had ten household servants, "beginning with the
number-one boy and ending with the number-three coolie," and including "the cook and the marmiton, and two amahs, known respectively as the 'wash-and-baby amah' and the 'sew-sew amah.'" In
addition, the legation servants included "four ma-fus, that is to say
the old stableman and his three sons (there is also a grandson who
looks after the baby's donkey, but I pay him). Then there is the
washerman and his help; the head gardener, four garden coolies,
and the k'ai-men-ti, or gate porter, and the tingchai, or letter
carrier."[11]

There were few automobiles in Peking before the 1920s or any motor roads to speak of. The foreign community was dependent upon its ponies for transportation to the racecourse (some four miles from Peking, burnt by the Boxers but rebuilt on a much grander scale), to picnics at the Summer Palace, and to the Western Hills. Where one did not go by pony, or carriage, one walked, as on the section of the south wall of the Tartar City between the Chienmen and Hatamen which had been handed over to the legations by the Boxer Protocol and was extensively used by foreigners as a promenade. It was patrolled by legation troops and no Chinese were permitted to walk on it. In the summer months everybody, except the Maritime Customs officials, sought refuge from the heat of Peking in the hills twelve miles west of the capital, especially at Pa-ta-chu, a place noted for its temples which the foreigners (and some Chinese dignitaries) rented for the summer. The foreigner, typical of his derogation of things Chinese, referred to the eight peaks with his own historical appellations: there was a "Mount Bruce" and a "Mount Burlingame." The more formal etiquette of the endless rounds of dinners, balls, and theatricals which filled the rest of the year was relaxed somewhat--although Sir John Jordan was known to dress in a dinner jacket with a black tie even when he ate alone in a rented Chinese temple on a hot summer evening--and excursions to the surrounding villages brought these European visitors as near as most ever came to contact with the daily life of the Chinese populace.

There was of course work as well as play. Between October 1900 and May 1920, the Diplomatic Body held 219 formal meetings-- omitting August 6, 1914 to August 23, 1917, from the outbreak of World War I until the Chinese declaration of war against Austria-Hungary and Germany, so as to avoid unpleasant confrontations between enemies. Collectively, the diplomats considered ad infinitum such matters as stamp dues, currency circulation, monetary crises, and other financial subjects; commerce, navigation, and treaty ports; affairs of the concessions and settlements; the Shanghai Mixed Court; rights and privileges of diplomatic and consular staffs; the revolution of 1911 and its aftermath; and--conspicuously--the management of the Legation Quarter itself. Individually, the representatives of the major powers with varying degrees of effectiveness sought to preserve or enhance the political and economic interests of their several nations in China and East Asia (inevitably at times in conflict with their fellows); and to represent, protect, and, occasionally unwillingly, attempt to float the schemes of their individual nationals resident in or visiting China.

Under the regime of extraterritoriality and the "unequal treaties," the Diplomatic Body and its consular subordinates in the treaty ports may be thought of, in effect, as acting as integral parts of the government of China itself. Each treaty power exercised exclusive civil and criminal jurisdiction over its own nationals in China, through its consuls and with its minister serving as appellate judge (except in the cases of the United States and Great Britain which provided special courts for the exercise of their extraterritorial jurisdictional rights). The ministers were aggressively alert against all real or imagined violations of the treaties--not only to their letter but to their spirit as well, which in the accumulated precedents of the decades since the Treaty of Nanking had come to be one of loose and generous interpretation of the rights of the treaty powers. There was little reluctance about the application of sufficient pressure at the Foreign Ministry and elsewhere whenever the status of foreigners and their interests might be affected by some act of the Chinese government. Cases of direct damage were pursued sedulously and modest compensation infrequently accepted. Officials "responsible" for these "outrages" were denounced freely. Attempts were made to obtain the suppression of publications allegedly abusive to foreigners with little more hesitation than requests for the removal of obstructions to traffic on the Yangtze or Pearl rivers. And much time and effort were spent in attacking the granting by the central or provincial governments, or the possibility thereof, of exclusive concessions or contracts to the representatives of some power other than one's own. "In European countries," former American minister Denby wrote in 1906, "his passport would be given him if he attempted to do a tithe of these things."[12]

Minister Denby also remarked that the minister to China (in the case of the United States allegedly because of the pressure of opinion at home as expressed in the "great newspapers") "is bound to assume that in all cases his countrymen are in the right and the Chinese are in the wrong. It is considered a very strong proof of mental weakness, or moral obliquity, if the minister dares to look into the right or the wrong of any question which is alleged to involve the substantial rights of his countrymen."[13] Perhaps with respect to such relatively minor matters as claims for individual damages, the minister might consult his conscience before he pressed the Chinese for compliance. But in the main arena, the policy of his government, whose premises he generally accepted, was at a minimum to compel the observance of the provisions of existing treaties. To this end

the powers might, as they saw it, legitimately dictate the internal
policy of China in so far as it affected foreigners. But this was
only the minimum, the self-styled correctness of those powers
whose agenda in China was primarily a commercial one and who,
with lapses justified by reference to the greater rapaciousness of
others, solemnly advocated the "open door" for the enterprise of all.

Individually or collectively, however, in matters both political
and economic, the diplomatic representatives of the great powers
probably were a good deal less effective than they thought they were
in achieving their larger ends, in influencing or controlling the decisions and actions of Chinese governments central and local. There
were too many ways in which late-Ch'ing and then republican officials
could procrastinate, dissemble, or in extremus resist openly even
against the importunities of a strong European nation. This resistance was fed by the steady penetration of nationalist consciousness
and aspirations for unconditional sovereignty first into the late-Ch'ing
bureaucracy and then more explicitly among their republican successors. The several lenders in the case of the Reorganization Loan
of 1913 might have believed that, by inserting a foreign Director of
the Bureau of National Loans into the disbursement process, they
would be in a position to influence how President Yuan Shih-k'ai
employed the proceeds. Indeed, the final loan agreement had been
stalled as the powers jockeyed to have their nationals appointed as
advisors and auditors. In practice, the foreign auditors and accountants learned only what Yuan found it convenient to apprise them of.

It was, I may suggest, frequently the foreign attitude toward
China, the assertion without any shame of large claims on the basis
of vague Chinese statements which were themselves forced by foreign
demands, that was fundamentally more derogatory of Chinese sovereignty than any practical gains accruing to the lucky concessionaires.
One instructive example is the insistence of the United States that
it be given participation in the projected Hukuang railroad loan in
1909. Chang Chih-tung had just about wrapped up a loan agreement
with German, British, and French banking groups in June 1909 when
(at the instigation of J. P. Morgan and Company, Kuhn, Loeb and
Company, the First National Bank of New York, and the National
City Bank of New York) a personal telegram arrived from President
Taft to Prince Ch'un, the Regent, demanding a piece of the loan for
the American banking group. The American case rested upon alleged
promises by the Chinese government in 1903 and 1904 to Edwin

Conger, the U.S. minister, that if Chinese capital were unable to finance the railroad from Hankow to Szechuan (now part of the proposed Hukuang system), United States and British capital would be given the first opportunity to bid for any foreign loan. On this basis, the Chinese were pressed relentlessly, and strong representations were made to Paris and London. But the pledges to Conger, which the Department of State described as "solemn obligations," did not exist!

In fact, in both 1903 and 1904 the Chinese Foreign Ministry had bluntly rejected requests by Conger on behalf of American firms, its reply of 1903, for example, concluding with this statement: "In short, when companies of various nationalities apply to China for railway concessions, it must always remain with China to decide the matter. It is not possible to regard an application not granted as conferring any rights or as being proof that thereafter application must first be made to the persons concerned." Even the texts of the 1903 exchanges were not available in Washington. The Department of State demanded in a cable to Peking in July 1909 that they be transmitted forthwith because they were needed to bolster negotiations in London. But, given their content, when they arrived the texts were not shown to the British. [14] China, in the end, acceded to the Taft telegram because of pressure, not because of the alleged "pledges." And the European banking group admitted the Americans to the loan consortium ultimately because they feared that it would be difficult to enforce their own quite shadowy loan guarantees in China if they now denied similar American claims. An agreement for a loan of £6 million was signed with the four-power consortium on May 20, 1911. In pursuit of whatever political and economic advantages it seemed to offer the lenders, China was to be treated as an object and not as an equal partner in commerce.

One significant source of diplomatic arrogance frequently noted was the language barrier. The principal foreign representatives in Peking--ministers, counselors, first secretaries, and the like--rarely knew Chinese. With honorable exceptions, the leading foreign merchants in the treaty ports were similarly innocent. As classes, the only foreigners who spoke Chinese were the official interpreters ("Chinese secretaries"), the commissioners of the Maritime Customs--Sir Robert Hart insisted on it--the missionaries, and the student interpreters attached to the legations who entered the consular service. And few of these went beyond a knowledge of the spoken colloquial to undertake to write the Chinese language. The

typical dependence of the foreigner upon his "boy" to interpret for
him left him usually in painless ignorance of the real character of
the individual Chinese with whom he dealt and of the deeper lying
currents of Chinese society.

At the consular level, the iceberg of the foreign diplomatic
establishment of which the Peking Diplomatic Body was only the tip,
the language situation was somewhat better.   In 1913 Great Britain
maintained consulates at twenty-eight ports as well as Peking.   Eight
of these were consulates-general with their more extensive staffs
(Canton, Chengtu, Hankow, Kashgar, Mukden, Shanghai--where the
British Supreme Court was also located, Tientsin, and Yunnan-fu).
Seven student interpreters were attached to the Peking legation in
that year.   The British consular service, in contrast to the American before well into the twentieth century, was a highly professional
body, recruited by competitive examination and in general destined
to a lifetime career in China.   Upon appointment as a student interpreter, the prospective consul embarked upon two years of intensive
study of Chinese in Peking, at the conclusion of which the results of
his language examination played an important part in determining his
future placement within the consular service.   The United States,
which in 1913 staffed five consulates-general (Canton, Hankow, Mukden, Shanghai, and Tientsin) and nine consulates, appointed its first
student interpreter only in 1902.   This was Julean Arnold, later
commercial attaché in Peking and the author of China: A Commercial and Industrial Handbook (1926).   In 1913 there were nine American student interpreters attached to the Peking legation, and among
the consuls a number were clearly "China specialists" including
Nelson T. Johnson at Changsha and Clarence E. Gauss at Shanghai
who were later each to serve as ambassador to China.   This was
clearly a change from the short-term political appointments and the
system of consular agents on a fee basis which were typical of the
era before World War I.

The pre-1917 Russian consular service was characterized by
an expertise akin to that of the British which drew on the skills of
the Faculty of Oriental Languages at the University of St. Petersburg
and ultimately on the fact that Russia had enjoyed facilities for language training in Peking since the eighteenth century.   In 1913 eight
consulates-general were maintained (Canton, Harbin, Kashgar, Mukden, Newchwang, Shanghai, Tientsin, and Peking) and eleven consulates (of which nine were in Manchuria or Mongolia).   Four student

interpreters were attached to the legation in that year. The sino-
logical competence of many of the Russian consuls may be illustrated
by the examples of the consul-general at Tientsin, Peter H. Tiedmann
(P— G— Tideman), a graduate in 1894 of the St. Petersburg Oriental
Faculty and a student interpreter during 1896-1899 before assuming
consular posts; and A— T— Beltchenko, consul at Hankow and also a
St. Petersburg Oriental Faculty graduate who had first arrived in
China in 1899. Beltchenko was the cotranslator into English in 1912
of Sovremennaia politicheskaia organizatziia Kitaia, first published
in Peking in 1910 by H. S. Brunnert (I— S— Brunnert), the Russian
legation's assistant Chinese secretary, and V. V. Hagelstrom (V—
V— Gagel'strom), secretary to the Shanghai consulate-general. The
English version, revised and enlarged by N— Th— Kolessoff, consul-
general and Chinese secretary at the Russian Peking legation, is of
course that indispensable handbook of all later scholars of modern
Chinese history, Present Day Political Organization of China.

Japan in 1913 maintained eight consulates-general (Canton,
Chientao, Hankow, Harbin, Mukden, Shanghai, Tientsin, and Hong
Kong) and twenty-two consulates of which ten were in Manchuria.
Within the Japanese consular service, appointments to posts in China
tended to be regarded as less desirable than service in European or
American missions. Before World War I, the language competence
of Japanese consular officers who allegedly saw their Chinese service as stepping stones to more attractive assignments elsewhere
was often criticized in the Diet. On the whole, however, the Japanese consular contingent was highly professional (recruited through
the higher civil service examination primarily from graduates of
the prestigious Tokyo and Kyoto Universities) and knowledgeable
about the China in which it served.

For the rest, Germany in 1913 staffed one consulate-general
and sixteen consulates; France, three consulates-general and ten
consulates; Austria-Hungary, three in all; Belgium, six; Italy, seven;
Mexico, four; the Netherlands, nine; Portugal, seven; and Spain,
seven, but usually in the charge of third country nationals. Canton,
Shanghai, Hankow and Tientsin were almost without exception consular posts for all the treaty powers, with the remainder of their
consular offices distributed to reflect the "spheres of influence"
which each claimed, e.g., Japan and Russia in Manchuria as already
noted, Great Britain heavily represented in cities along the Yangtze
River, and France in southwest China.

III. MISSIONARIES

In common with the other nationals of the treaty powers, the treaties of 1842 and 1844 gave to missionaries the right to reside in the treaty ports. Imperial edicts in 1844 and 1845 extended official toleration to Chinese Christians, but until the treaties of 1858-1860 missionaries were prohibited from entering the interior of China for the purposes of proselytization. The 1858 treaties made toleration a specific treaty obligation, in effect placing both missionaries and Chinese Christians under the protection of foreign powers, but gave to missionaries no other privileges not accorded to foreigners in general. The special right of missionaries to reside permanently in the interior, to purchase or lease land, and to erect buildings rested on the anomalous Chinese text of Article VI of the Sino-French treaty of 1860.

Like the other treaties of these years the foreign-language text, in this case French, was declared authoritative; it contained only a reconfirmation of a prior imperial edict ordering the return of confiscated French religious properties. The Chinese text, however, added the sentence, "It is, in addition, permitted to French missionaries to rent and purchase land in all the provinces, and to erect buildings thereon at pleasure." Spurious as their strict legal claim might be, the French insisted upon it and forced formal Chinese assent in the "Berthemy Convention" of 1865. By the most-favored-nation clauses of the treaties this sentence extended to missionaries of all nationalities the right to establish themselves and their mission stations far from the treaty ports to which other foreigners were restricted.

In the early republic missionaries and "merchants" were the largest groups among the European foreigners temporarily resident in China who were identified by common purposes. Protected by the general extraterritorial provisions of the treaties, their omnipresence sanctioned by Article VI, Catholic or Protestant missionaries reached into nearly every corner of the country. As of 1919, all but 106 out of 1,704 hsien in China proper and Manchuria reported some Protestant evangelical activity. Unlike the foreign merchants, missionaries frequently learned the Chinese language and of necessity were in relatively close daily contact with the Chinese to whom their evan-

gelical message was addressed. Their broadest goals stressed
evenhandedly individual salvation through conversion to Christ and
the firm organization of a Chinese church. By the early 1920s
many (Protestants at least) had begun to see that the manifold activities of the foreign missionaries had failed to create a strong
indigenous church, in fact that the very extent of the foreign presence was a major obstacle to that achievement. The executive
secretary of the interdenominational China Continuation Committee,
E. C. Lobenstine, wrote in his introduction to that Committee's
magistral survey of Protestant missionary activity in China:

> The coming period is expected to be one of transition,
> during which the burden of the work and its control will
> increasingly shift from the foreigner to the Chinese.
> The rising tide of national consciousness within Chris-
> tian circles is leading to a profound dissatisfaction with
> certain aspects of the present situation on the part of
> many of the ablest and most consecrated Chinese Chris-
> tians. They have a very intense and rightful desire
> that Christianity shall be freed from the incubus of
> being regarded as a "foreign religion" and that the de-
> nominational divisions of the West be not perpetuated
> permanently in China. They regard the predominance
> of foreign influence in the Church as one of the chief
> hindrances to a more rapid spread of Christianity in
> China, and feel that it is indirectly responsible for
> many of the weaknesses of the Church. One of the
> more prominent younger Chinese recently voiced the
> opinion in the Chinese Recorder, "that missionary work,
> excellent as it is, has not succeeded in creating in the
> Chinese Christian the sense of proprietorship in the
> work of the Church." This is unfortunately only too
> true, and it must be the main task of the years imme-
> diately ahead to see that such a sense of proprietorship
> is created and that the Church becomes truly indigenous
> in China. [1]

Only to a limited extent was the task set by Reverend Lobenstine
accomplished before the extinction of the Christian church in China
after 1949. Missionaries and communicants increased in number,
more Chinese were recruited into the church leadership, the quality
of educational and medical services was improved. But for the

most part the Christian missionary component of the foreign establishment in China was not much different in character in the twenty-
five years after 1922 from what it was in the first two decades of
the twentieth century.

The flourishing of the missionary "occupation" in the first
quarter of the twentieth century, it may be said, was a brief inter-
lude bounded at one end by the Boxer uprising and by the burgeoning
of a virulent nationalism hostile to Christianity as an emanation of
foreign imperialism on the other. In the immediate post-Boxer
years Protestant Christianity in China prospered because after more
than a half century of mediocre results it forged a temporary link
with the domestic forces of reform which had a use for it. To the
development of modern education in the last Ch'ing decade, and in
the first decade of the republic, the expanding missionary schools
contributed much at a time when indigenous facilities and teachers
were in short supply. Modern Western medicine in China was to
an important degree a consequence of missionary demonstration and
instruction. "Young China" of the 1910s and 1920s was frequently
the product of missionary schools--the new urban patriots and reformers, the leaders in such new professions as scientific agriculture, journalism, and sociology. But it was a doubly ambiguous
linkage upon which the prosperity of the Protestant missionary enterprise depended. The Kuomintang regime with which it eventually
became identified--that was natural enough, both were essentially
urban-based, both variations on the theme of "modernization"
bourgeois-style--tolerated rather than encouraged it. Even conservative nationalism, as Reverend Lobenstine acknowledged, accepted
for the long run only a truly indigenous church. And by being urban
and nonpolitical, in practice stressing the salvation of the individual
within the existing political system, Christianity was necessarily
increasingly distant from the growing rumblings of social revolution
in the countryside which would in 1949 bring to an end the brief
domination of China's revolution by the semi-Westernized urban
elite to whom the missionary effort was wedded.

The period 1900-1920 saw a substantial growth in all aspects
of the "Christian occupation of China," the unfortunate but telling
words with which the Protestant missionaries described their activities.[2] Table 2 summarizes the essential information for the Protestant missions.

TABLE 2

GROWTH OF THE PROTESTANT CHURCH IN CHINA

	1889	1906	1919
Foreign missionaries	1,296	3,833	6,636
Ordained Chinese	211	345	1,065
Total Chinese workers	1,657	9,961	24,732
Communicants claimed	37,287	178,251	345,853
Students enrolled in missionary schools	16,836	57,683	212,819

Roman Catholic missions in China expanded rapidly in the post-Boxer years. In 1901, 1,075 foreign and 500 Chinese priests served a Catholic community estimated at 721,000 communicants. By 1920 there were 1,500-2,000 European priests, approximately 1,000 Chinese priests, 1,000 foreign nuns, 1,900 Chinese nuns, a claimed 2,000,000 communicants, 13,000 Chinese catechists and teachers, and 180,000 students enrolled in Catholic schools. Among the thirteen or more Catholic missionary societies, those of French origin (Lazarists, Missions Etrangères de Paris, for example) were especially prominent, reflecting the French claim to a protectorate over the Catholic church in China based on the toleration clauses of the treaties. More than half of the foreign priests in China on the eve of World War I were French nationals. The Catholic effort was formally organized into fifty-one "vicariats et préfectures apostoliques" which divided among themselves all of the provinces of China. Approximately fifteen hundred locations were staffed by foreign or Chinese priests, with the largest numbers of Catholics located in Chihli, Kiangsu, Szechwan, and Shantung. While they were also present in the larger cities where the Protestants were concentrated, the Catholics emphasized work in the more rural areas, sought the conversion of entire families or villages, attempted to build integrated local Catholic communities, and tended to restrict their educational efforts to the children of converts only. Prior to the 1920s the Catholic missions did not undergo a major expansion of educational and medical activities comparable to the post-Boxer Protestant effort. Any desire to have a broader impact on Chinese society was decidedly secondary to the saving of souls. Anti-Christian movements in the 1920s, in contrast to the nineteenth-century missionary cases, were directed more frequently against the Protestants, an indication that Catholicism remained apart from the main currents that were shaping twentieth-century China.

With the exception of the fundamentalist China Inland Mission and its associated societies, after 1900 Protestant missionaries gradually shifted their emphasis from a predominant concern with the conversion of individuals to the broadened goal of Christianizing all of Chinese society. This implied an increasing investment of personnel and funds in educational and medical work in order to realize, as one missionary leader wrote, "the social implications" of the Gospel. The effort was flawed, however, by the concentration of the Protestant church in the more developed eastern coastal provinces and the largest cities. That part of Chinese society which was predominantly rural was less deeply touched by the missionaries' exertions.

The 6,636 Protestant missionaries as of 1919 were resident in 693 locations in all the provinces of China where they staffed 1,037 separate mission stations. Of the 693 residential centers, 578 (83 percent) were occupied by only one mission society, and 442 (65 percent) had five or fewer missionaries in residence. These more sparsely settled locations tended to be in the interior provinces. Fifty-seven percent of the missionaries were located in the coastal provinces, 26 percent in the Yangtze valley provinces, and only 17 percent away from the east coast and the Yangtze valley. The eight residential centers of Shanghai, Peking, Canton, Nanking, Foochow, Changsha, Chengtu, and Tsinan each had more than one hundred missionaries and together accounted for 26 percent of the total foreign personnel. Two-thirds of the Protestant missionaries and one-quarter of the claimed communicants resided in 176 cities with estimated populations of fifty thousand or more where perhaps 6 percent of China's total population lived. In order of precedence, the seven coastal provinces of Kwangtung, Fukien, Chekiang, Kiangsu, Shantung, Chihli, and Fengtien accounted for 71 percent of the Protestant communicants, 63 percent of lower primary students, and 77 percent of middle school students. To be sure, evangelistic activity-- sometimes fitful, in other circumstances well-organized--radiated out from the residential centers. In fact, 6,391 "congregations" and 8,886 "evangelistic centers" were claimed in 1919. But most were only a few li from the urban mission station.

From 61 separate Protestant missionary societies in 1900, the number increased to 130 in 1920, to which must be added 36 Christian organizations such as the YMCA, the Salvation Army, and the Yale-in-China mission which were not organized on a denominational basis. This increase was the consequence of the arrival in China after 1900 of many small sectarian societies, many of them American. The largest new mission to begin work in this period was that of the Seventh Day Adventists. In 1905 one-half of the foreign force was British (including the United Kingdom, Canada, Australia, and New Zealand), one-third American, and the rest from the European continent. By 1920, the British and American proportions had been reversed, the Americans now accounting for one-half of the Protestant missionaries in China. The Catholic missionary effort was overwhelmingly European in personnel and control, American Catholic missionaries arriving in China mainly after 1920. Table 3 shows the relative strengths of the major Protestant denominations without regard to nationality.

TABLE 3

RELATIVE STRENGTHS OF PROTESTANT DENOMINATIONS, 1919

		Number of			
	Societies	Missionaries	Stations	Communicants	Hospitals
Anglican	4	635	79	19,114	39
Baptist	9	588	68	44,367	31
Congregational	4	345	34	25,816	32
Lutheran	18	590	116	32,209	23
Methodist	8	946	83	74,004	63
Presbyterian	12	1,080	96	79,199	92
China Inland Mission	12	960	246	50,541	17
Others	63	1,492	315	20,603	29
Totals	130	6,636	1,037	345,853	326

From the first decade of the twentieth century, while denominational distinctions were continued and within them the separate identities of the individual societies, Protestant Christianity in China displayed tendencies toward formulating a common, basic theology and substantial efforts for organizational unity in some spheres of activity. The irrelevance of confessional distinctions linked to a European past which was largely unknown in China furnished an incentive for modifying and simplifying theologies imported from abroad. The China Centenary Missionary Conference of 1907 adopted a collective theological stance which in later years continued to provide doctrinal guidelines for all but the more fundamentalist Protestant societies such as the China Inland Mission. Organizationally, the larger societies joined in publishing the major Protestant monthly magazine, the Chinese Recorder; supported nondenominational or interdenominational literature societies; participated in the China Christian Educational Association, the China Medical Missionary Association, and the China Sunday School Union; founded union theological schools and interdenominational colleges and universities; participated in all-China missionary conferences in 1877, 1890, and 1907, and in the National Christian Conference in 1922 which also formally included the Chinese church for the first time. A major expression of Protestant unity was the China Continuation Committee of 1913-1922 which was succeeded by the National Christian Council in 1922, once more to enlarge the formal role of the Chinese church within the Christian establishment. Accommodation and cooperation were never, of course, completely effective. The conservative China Inland Mission, for example, withdrew from the National Christian Council in 1926. But where the Protestant missionary effort succeeded--or failed--it was at least perceived as doing so in one body.

The largest Protestant missionary societies, ranked by the number of missionaries maintained in the field as of 1919, are listed in Table 4, which also shows the number of mission stations and the geographical field of each major society.[3] These eighteen societies together accounted for 4,350 (66 percent of the total) missionaries and 611 (59 percent of the total) mission stations. An "average" mission station might be staffed by six or seven missionaries, but the actual distribution varied greatly from a frequent four or less for the China Inland Mission and the Christian and Missionary Alliance to averages of fourteen or fifteen for the Board of Foreign Missions of the Methodist Episcopal Church, the American Presbyterian Mission, North, and the American Board of Commissioners for Foreign Missions. In general, concentration of missionaries at one station was an indication of extensive educational and medical efforts as well

TABLE 4

THE LARGEST PROTESTANT MISSIONARY SOCIETIES, 1919

	Nationality	Number of Missionaries	Stations	Location of Mission Stations
China Inland Mission and Affiliates	Int.	960	246	An, Che, Chi, Ho, Hun, Hup, Kan, Ki, Ku, Kwei, Sha, She, Sung, Sze, Yün, Man, Sin
American Presbyterian Mission, North	U.S.	502	36	An, Che, Chi, Hun, Ku, Sung, Tung, Yün
Board of Foreign Missions of the Methodist Episcopal Church	U.S.	419	28	An, Chi, Fu, Ki, Ku, Sung, Sze
Church Missionary Society	Br.	353	58	Che, Fu, Hun, Ku, Si, Tung, Sze, Yün
Protestant Episcopal Church, U.S.A.	U.S.	202	15	An, Hun, Hup, Ki, Ku
American Board of Commissioners for Foreign Missions	U.S.	198	14	Chi, Fu, Sha, Sung, Tung
YMCA	Int.	192	24	Major Cities
American Baptist Foreign Mission Society (Northern Baptist)	U.S.	188	19	Che, Ki, Ku, Tung, Sze

Organization				
Missionary Society of the Methodist Church of Canada	Br.	184	10	Sze
Foreign Mission Board of the Southern Baptist Convention	U.S.	175	24	An, Ho, Ku, Si, Tung, Sung
American Presbyterian Mission, South	U.S.	146	15	Che, Ku, Sung
London Missionary Society	Br.	145	17	Chi, Fu, Hup, Ku, Tung
Seventh-Day Adventist Missionary Board	U.S.	138	21	Che, Chi, Fu, Ho, Hun, Hup, Ku, She, Si, Sung, Sze, Tung, Man
Baptist Missionary Society (English)	Br.	123	11	Sha, She, Sung
Methodist Episcopal Mission, South	U.S.	118	6	Che, Ku
Wesleyan Methodist Missionary Society	Br.	118	19	Hun, Hup, Si, Tung
Christian and Missionary Alliance	U.S.	106	25	An, Hun, Hup, Kan, Ku, Si
Church Missions in Many Lands (Brethren)	Br.	83	23	Ki, Sung, Mon

Key
An	Anhwei	Ho	Hopei	Ki	Kiangsi	She	Shensi	Tung	Kwangtung
Che	Chekiang	Hun	Hunan	Ku	Kiangsu	Si	Kwangsi	Yün	Yünnan
Chi	Chihli	Hup	Hupei	Kwei	Kweichou	Sung	Shantung	Man	Manchuria
Fu	Fukien	Kan	Kansu	Sha	Shansi	Sze	Szechwan	Mon	Mongolia
								Sin	Sinkiang

as evangelism, while dispersion to smaller stations reflected a primary if not exclusive emphasis on spreading the Gospel. As another indicator of the different emphases of the several societies, the China Inland Mission, for example, employed 66 percent of its Chinese staff in evangelical work, 30 percent in education, and 4 percent in medical work, while the comparable figures for the American Board of Commissioners for Foreign Missions were 28 percent in evangelism, 64 percent in education, and 8 percent in medical work.

Much of the "mission-centric" outlook of the Protestant missionary in the late-Ch'ing persisted into the republic. "From the time they arrived in China until the time they left," Paul Cohen has written of the former period, "the missionaries lived and worked in the highly organized structure of the mission compound, which resulted in their effective segregation--psychological as well as physical--from the surrounding Chinese society. This segregation was only partly imposed by the Chinese; it was also self-imposed. For the missionaries really did not want to enter the Chinese world any more than they had to. Their whole purpose was to get the Chinese to enter theirs."[4] With segregation went an absolute self-righteousness about their calling which overrode any possible moral qualms against justifying, even calling for, the employment of gunboats and troops by their home governments to settle the numerous antimissionary incidents which punctuated their period of residence in China. Even those of a more liberal theology and a tentative commitment to the Social Gospel, because they saw the conservative bureaucracy and the traditional social elites as the principal barriers both to the conversion of China and to the modernization of her society, were not reluctant to "bless China" with "a much needed lesson" in response to even minor riots directed against themselves or their converts. The high point--or low point morally--of missionary bloodthirstiness came in the aftermath of the Boxer uprising. Understandable, perhaps, in light of the losses which many suffered and the dangers experienced, but also to bear bitter fruit by enhancing the indentification of "God's work" with the depredations of imperialist aggression.[5]

Yet the two post-Boxer decades saw some changes both in the relationship of many Protestant missionaries to the society which surrounded them and in the eagerness with which they sought armed intervention to protect their special status. Their attitude of cultural superiority, galling even to Chinese Christians, remained, but increasing numbers of Protestant missionaries moved beyond the

evangelical limits of the nineteenth-century mission compound to par-
ticipate actively in educational, medical, and philanthropic work,
joining the reform currents of the early twentieth century.   Education
for women (Ginling College in Nanking was founded in 1915), the anti-
footbinding movement, attention to urban and labor problems by the
YMCAs (of small effect since they depended for their financial support and legitimacy on the urban wealthy), famine relief, public
health (anti-TB drives, antifly campaigns), public playgrounds and
athletic and recreational programs, the anti-opium movement, and
the scientific study of agriculture (by the School of Agriculture and
Forestry of the University of Nanking)--these were some of the areas
in which Protestant missionaries took the lead or were notably involved.

Antimissionary riots, while they occurred sporadically, were
noticeably fewer in the years after 1900.   This was perhaps one
reason for the decline in the eagerness with which missionaries
called for the dispatch of gunboats.   Also at work was an increasing
feeling that, now that China gave evidence of being capable of reforming herself, it was less necessary for the powers to intervene to
force the pace of change.   American missionaries in particular enthu-
siastically welcomed the overthrow of the Manchus and viewed the
new republic whose president promised religious freedom as almost
their own creation.   Leading Protestant missionaries strongly supported China against Japan at the time of the Twenty-one Demands
and in 1919 when the Versailles conference failed to restore Chinese
sovereignty in Shantung.   But not until the mid-1920s, beyond the
framework of this essay, did a substantial part of the Protestant
missionaries perceive the strength of Chinese nationalism and the
potential danger to their enterprise of reliance on the toleration
clauses and the extraterritorial rights of the treaties.   Nor were a
majority of the missionaries, in spite of the urgings of some (as in
the statement by E. C. Lobenstine quoted earlier), willing to surren-
der their de facto control of all Christian institutions in China.

The mission station, a walled compound owned or leased by the
missionary society and protected by extraterritoriality, remained the
most typical feature of the missionary "occupation" of China.   Within
the enclosure, which inevitably displayed the British or American
national flag, were the residences of the missionaries, the church,
the school or classrooms, and the hospital or dispensary.   As I have
already suggested, the typical station was located in a substantial

urban area. At some distance from the compound a few street chapels were kept open for part of each afternoon and staffed by a foreign missionary and his native helper. "Outstation" communities of converts, where they had been organized, were served by native pastors and visited several times a year by the staff of the mission station. These were rarely off the beaten track.

The station staff of two or three missionary families and a number of single women might include a physician or nurse on the average in one station out of three, although the actual distribution of medical workers was uneven with a concentration in Kwangtung, Szechwan, Fukien, Kiangsu, Chihli, and Shantung. Of the 6,636 Protestant missionaries reported in 1919, 2,495 (38 percent) were men of whom 1,310 were ordained; 2,202 (33 percent) were married women; and 1,939 (29 percent) were single women. Physicians numbered 348 men and 116 women; and 206 of the women were trained nurses. The ordained men were responsible for the primary evangelical task of the mission and filled the vocal leadership roles. Many of the unordained men were teachers in the expanding network of missionary schools; the women were occupied in teaching and nursing and carried out much of the visitation in Chinese homes

The principal medium for evangelization was preaching, in the mission church and in the street chapels, an endeavor whose success depended at least in part on the missionary's ability to use colloquial Chinese. Before 1910 the only organized language schools for Protestant missionaries were run by the China Inland Mission at Yangchow and Anking, this last dating back to 1887. Language instruction was ad hoc at each mission station and poor command of Chinese continued to be a serious problem for many. By the early years of the republic, however, a number of substantial union (interdenominational) language schools were in operation employing modern "phonetic inductive" methods and graded texts. The China Inland Mission maintained "training homes" at Chinkiang and Yangchow which provided a six-month basic course using the Reverend F. W. Baller's primer and Chinese teachers. Approximately 150 students representing twenty different societies were enrolled annually in the Department of Missionary Training of the University of Nanking which since 1912 offered a one-year residential course staffed by 51 Chinese teachers. A second year program was available, but most students continued with correspondence courses in succeeding years. The North China Union Language School, formally orga-

nized in 1913 and affiliated with Yenching University in 1920, enrolled
147 students in 1921 and offered a program similar to Nanking's.
Other schools were the Union Missionary Training School in Chengtu,
part of West China Union University; the Wu Dialect School of Soochow University in Shanghai; and the Canton Union Language School.
Few missionaries, like few diplomats, ever attained a full proficiency
in written Chinese, but some command of the spoken colloquial was
widespread.

Almost every mission station supported a lower primary school.
Of the 693 Protestant residential centers, 306 reported higher primary schools, and 141 middle schools. The number of schools at
each level and the enrollments in 1919 are shown in Table 5, which
also gives the estimated enrollments in government schools in 1916.

TABLE 5

PROTESTANT MISSIONARY SCHOOLS AND ENROLLMENTS, 1919

	Number of Mission Schools	Enrollment in Mission Schools Boys/Girls/Total	Enrollment in Government Schools--1916
Lower primary	5,637	103,232/48,350/151,582	3,752,982
Higher primary	962	23,490/ 9,409/ 32,899	388,941
Middle	291	12,644/ 2,569/ 15,213	179,621*

*Including equivalent technical and normal schools

These figures may all be only guesses--the mission enrollments are
fewer than those shown in Table 2--but the proportions are probably
not much askew. They indicate that mission lower primary school
pupils were only 4 percent as many as those in government schools,
but that at the higher and middle school levels the proportion increased to over 8 percent. In more advanced education, and this
will be even truer at the university level to be discussed presently,
the missionary role was relatively larger than at the basic level.
In the period 1907-1920, the number of mission school students--

perhaps one-half of whom came from Christian families--quadrupled while Protestant communicants only doubled in number, suggesting both a conscious missionary effort to reach China's youth and the lure of modern education in the late-Ch'ing and early republic. Protestant missionaries frequently boasted that while overall only one in seventy-five of Chinese children of school age was receiving an education, one in three of all Christian youth was enrolled in a mission school. Again, the figures may be inexact, but the proportions are telling not just about the higher educational levels of Christian communicants, but also as a reflection of the urban concentration of the missionaries and their converts. There were few modern schools in the rural areas.

The Protestant mission schools were staffed not only by foreign teachers, who were more in evidence at the higher primary and middle school levels, but also by perhaps eight thousand male and three thousand female Chinese teachers. Lower primary schools were often primitive one-room establishments sorely lacking in books and equipment. The upper schools enjoyed somewhat better facilities. They frequently used English as a medium of instruction--which permitted not a few missionaries to avoid the necessity to learn Chinese and swelled the number of male unordained missionaries--and, first by choice and then, from 1925, in order to qualify for government registration, followed curricula similar to those established by the Ministry of Education for government schools. All the mission middle schools taught some religious subjects; Chinese language and literature courses employed the "National Readers" of the Ministry; science teaching was poor in most schools, laboratory and demonstration equipment being expensive and in short supply; and few offered any vocational training. They were probably not any worse than the government middle schools, but the indications are that the mission middle school effort in the early republic had overextended itself given the plant, equipment, and staff that it could readily finance.

In higher education, twenty Protestant colleges and one Catholic school were in existence in 1920. The Protestant institutions, through reorganization and amalgamation, eventually formed the thirteen Christian colleges whose heyday was in the 1930s. Two additional Catholic colleges were organized later in the 1920s. In addition to these liberal arts schools, the Protestant missionary movement maintained a number of theological schools, some on a union basis, and several Christian medical colleges, and the Catholics a number of seminaries.

Except for West China Union University in Chengtu, where Canadian
and British personnel and organizational patterns were dominant,
the Protestant liberal arts colleges were largely the undertaking of
American missionaries who sought to create in China replicas of
the small denominational colleges of midwestern America from which
many had themselves graduated. Most had their beginnings in secondary schools founded in the later decades of the nineteenth century
which were gradually expanded and upgraded academically with the
intention of training a Chinese pastorate and teachers for the mission schools.

In 1920 the Protestant colleges together enrolled 2,017 students;
after a period of rapid growth in the early 1920s that total reached
3,500 in 1925. Total college enrollment in 1925 was approximately
21,000, the Protestant schools therefore accounting for 12 percent
and the thirty-four government institutions for 88 percent of the students. Even the largest of the Christian colleges--Yenching University
in Peking, St. John's in Shanghai, the University of Nanking, Shantung
Christian University in Tsinan--had no more than three or four hundred students. The size and disciplinary competence of the faculties
were similarly limited. In 1920 foreign teachers totalled 265, and
Chinese--most of them tutors--229. But many also taught in the
middle schools located on the same campuses.

Chartered in the United States, without any formal standing in
China until forced to apply for official registration by the Nationalist
government, controlled in fact by the absentee mission boards which
supplied two-thirds of their finances and intervened in the selection
of teachers, the Christian colleges were nearly self-contained foreign
enclaves in the period I am considering. Before the 1930s, probably
only St. John's, Yenching, and the University of Nanking offered
instruction at an academic level comparable to American undergrad-
uate schools. Of necessity most of their students came from graduates of the mission middle schools where alone sufficient English
was taught to prepare students to follow the English-language instruction which was used in all courses except Chinese literature and
philosophy. The attraction of some of the colleges (and of the mission middle schools) to Chinese students came to depend heavily on
their excellent training in English which provided for urban youth an
entree into the treaty port world of business and finance, or access
to government positions (in the telegraph, railway, or customs administrations, for example) where knowledge of a foreign language
was a significant asset. Of the 2,474 graduates as of 1920, 361 had

become ministers and others teachers, as the missionary founders had intended, but less than half of those enrolled in the first two decades of the twentieth century completed their courses. For most of the "dropouts" it was a command of English rather than a Christian liberal arts education which was the lure.

The Christian colleges did not escape the nationalist torrent of the late-1920s, a confrontation which goes beyond the scope of this essay.[6] In the 1930s they were increasingly secularized in their curricula and sinified in their faculties and administration. But the foreign identification was inescapable; none of these schools survived in China after 1949.

Both the missionaries' educational efforts and their medical work remained a source of contention within the Protestant movement in China even after the comity displayed at the Centenary Conference of 1907. The nineteenth-century mission schools were organized primarily to provide religious instruction to children of converts and offered only rudimentary exposure to secular knowledge. By the first part of the twentieth century increasing numbers of missionaries saw their teaching as more than a preface to preaching. They came to identify their religious message with the humanitarian and material achievements of pre-World War I Western civilization as a whole and saw the purpose of God not only in individual salvation but also in the total reconstitution of Chinese society in the image of their own. Americans like Young J. Allen (1836-1907)--translator, editor of the Wan-kuo kung-pao ("Review of the Times," 1875-1883, 1889-1907) devoted to interpreting the West to China, founder of the Anglo-Chinese College in Shanghai--took the lead in this broadening of the missionary purpose. Among the British Protestants, Timothy Richard (1845-1919) and the Society for the Diffusion of Christian Knowledge led the effort to reach the Chinese elite with the message of the Christian basis of Western secular achievements. Others of similar outlook included the Americans W. A. P. Martin (1827-1916), whose enormous literary output included many works in Chinese on international law, natural science, and Christianity; and Gilbert Reid (1857-1927), who broke with the Presbyterian mission to launch his own International Institute of China which aimed at an intellectual approach to the Chinese upper classes. Among those Protestant missionaries directly responsible for the educational efforts of their missions, such men as D. Z. Sheffield (1841-1913) of the American Board of Commissioners for Foreign Missions, presi-

dent of the North China Union College, one of the predecessors to
Yenching University; F. L. Hawks Pott (1864-1947), for fifty-two
years head of the American Protestant Episcopal Church's St.
John's University; and the Presbyterian Calvin Mateer (1836-1908), founder
of Shantung Christian University, thought along similar lines, although
they were less overtly "radical" in their theology than such indepen-
dents as Reid or Richards. But an easy accommodation between the
evangelistic and the broader educational purposes of the mission
higher schools was not to be expected, because home mission boards
were generally more conservative than missionaries in the field,
because the fundamentalist missions in China were powerful and
critical, and because funds and workers were always in short supply.

The situation in medical work was a similar one. Many medical
missionaries in the nineteenth century thought of themselves first
as evangelists and secondarily as physicians. Treatment in mission
dispensaries and hospitals was planned to give the patient a surfeit
of exposure to the Gospel. Gradually an increasing professionalism
developed, reflecting changes of outlook comparable to those which
inspired educational professionalism. Missionary hospitals grew in
number while the dosage of direct evangelism was decreased. In
1919, 240 out of 693 Protestant residential centers reported the
operation of a total of 326 hospitals. On the average they were
small facilities with 51 beds apiece, the total beds being 16,737.
Staffing these hospitals were 464 foreign physicians, 206 foreign
nurses, and some 2,600 Chinese medical workers only a small part
of whom were professionals. Like other parts of the missionary
establishment, the hospitals were located in urban areas and concentrated in the eastern coastal provinces. As the above data indicate, trained medical personnel were spread very thin among these
facilities; very few had more than one missionary doctor regularly
in residence. With honorable exceptions, they were useful but primitive institutions, lacking modern operating room equipment and labora-
tories, plagued by inadequate sterilization, and facing nearly insuper-
able problems with kitchens and latrines.

Western-type medical education in China began as an outgrowth
of missionary medical work, developing from informal training of
assistants by overworked doctors to eleven small, rudimentarily
staffed and equipped medical colleges, eight for men and three for
women, in 1913. Only the Peking Union Medical College, which
was taken over by the China Medical Board of the Rockefeller Foun-

dation in 1915 and formally ceased to be a missionary institution, approximated the standards of a Western medical school. The reorganized PUMC, small in size--only 166 students received M.D. degrees through 1936--and attacked by its critics for its isolation from the medical needs of China's rural masses, did become a training and research institution of international calibre. With PUMC setting the standards, the level of medical instruction in a number of the other schools improved in the 1920s and 1930s, but many of these pioneers were surpassed by the government medical schools at Peking University and in Shanghai.

While preaching was the favored means of missionary evangelization, the printed word was not neglected. A "Classified Index to the Chinese Literature of the Protestant Churches in China" issued in 1918 listed 1,188 books, 1,152 pamphlets, and 1,066 folded and sheet tracts as having been published through that year under Protestant auspices. While these works included a considerable amount of duplication, e.g., hymn books and catechisms, and sales of many titles were small, in the years 1915-1918 average annual sales were 633,746 books and 751,873 pamphlets. These included, as examples, 1,524 titles--original works and translations--in religion, 168 in history and geography, 149 each in literature and sociology, 109 in science, and 103 in medicine. The Presbyterian Mission Press, the largest, which had been established in Shanghai in 1844, published two million copies of Chinese-language works in 1920 of which one quarter were Scriptures, and 200,000 copies of English and bilingual works.

Nineteenth-century Protestant missionaries undertook many whole or partial translations of the Bible into classical Chinese beginning with Morrison's 1823 version, as well as numerous colloquial versions some of which were in romanization. In 1890 a conference of Protestant missionaries decided to produce a standard translation, a project which took nearly thirty years to complete. An "Easy Wenli" version of the New Testament appeared in 1908; and complete classical and Mandarin colloquial translations were published in 1919. Total sales of the Scriptures in the decade 1911-1920 were 316,566 complete Bibles, 1,170,221 New Testaments, and 56,677,101 biblical portions, these last largely hawked by colporteurs. A partial translation of the Bible from the Vulgate text had been made by Catholic missionaries, but there was, as might be expected, little emphasis on scriptural translations, Catholic

works distributed in China in Chinese and in European languages
tending to lives of the saints and defenses of the faith.

Protestant-sponsored newspapers and periodicals numbered fifty-
seven in 1921, of which half were monthly magazines and one a daily
paper.   Fifteen were published in Shanghai and seven in Canton.
Their quality in general was not very high, but perhaps good enough
for the mission propaganda, appeals to young people, church news,
theological discussions, and commentaries on the practical application of Christianity which filled their pages.   In the same year fifteen Catholic periodicals of all sorts were published, three in Chinese and nine in French (including the daily L'Echo de Chine in
Shanghai).

Withall, the identification of Christianity in China with the
foreign powers who had imposed the unequal treaties by force, the
eager participation of the missionaries and their converts in the
special privileges guaranteed by the treaties, remained the Achilles
heel of the missionary effort.   Extraterritoriality--even the tiniest
chapel flew a national flag--residence in the interior, intervention
in lawsuits and property disputes on behalf of their communicants,
acceptance and justification of the use of force, a demeaning attitude
of moral superiority which took away with one hand the virtues it
ascribed to the Chinese with the other--all these antagonized not
only the anti-Christian nationalist but also a growing number of
Chinese Christians.   But perhaps it is misleading to emphasize the
nationalist and anti-imperialist opposition which it aroused as the
principal shortcoming of the missionary effort in twentieth-century
China.   Was it not even more the case that, apart from a small
number of converts who were in truth deeply moved, where Christianity fundamentally failed was in its inability to affect either the
inner intellectual and cultural life of the Chinese nation or the movement of political and social forces which, oblivious to the missionaries
or any foreigner autonomously shaped China's modern history?   What
need was there for Christianity, a foreign and heterodox creed, in
a new world to be governed by science and political organization?

IV. MARITIME CUSTOMS, POST OFFICE, SALT ADMINISTRATION

The foreign presence in China in the first part of the twentieth century was highly visible in three departments of the central government which, while formally subordinated to Chinese authority, in many respects operated with de facto autonomy under the leadership of foreigners and with substantial foreign staffs in the more critical subordinate positions: the Maritime Customs Service, the Post Office, and the Salt Administration. By extending the system of foreign inspectors elaborated at Shanghai in 1853-1854 to the other treaty ports, Rule X of the "Rules of Trade" appended to the 1858 Treaty of Tientsin with Great Britain laid the basis for a foreign-dominated Maritime Customs whose semi-independence was not curbed until the nationalist upsurge of the 1920s. China's modern postal service grew up gradually under the auspices of the Maritime Customs, was formally recognized as a distinct agency by imperial edict in 1896, but remained under Customs administration until May 1911 when the Post Office, still to be headed by a foreign Postmaster-General, was transferred to the jurisdiction of the Ministry of Posts and Communications. The reorganized Salt Administration of the republican era, whose essential new feature was a foreign-controlled inspectorate on the model of the Maritime Customs, was a product of Article V of the "Reorganization Loan" agreement of 1913.

Both the Customs and the new Salt Administration, by enforcing a uniform tariff whose collection was certified by foreign customs commissioners or salt inspectors, substantially enlarged the revenues nominally under the control of the central government. But the domestic political context of the second half of the nineteenth century in which the Customs system was elaborated differed radically from that of the early years of the Chinese republic. Only briefly after 1911 was there a government in Peking with enough power to make an effective claim on the increased salt revenue collections. If the Maritime Customs revenue was a major prop sustaining the Ch'ing dynasty after the mid-nineteenth century time of troubles, the salt gabelle could do no more than maintain the shadow of power for successive Peking governments after the death of Yuan Shih-k'ai in 1916. And subsequent to the hypothecation of the customs revenue to service foreign loans forced on China by the disastrous war with Japan in 1894-1895 and then, after 1900, the enormous Boxer Indemnity, that "major prop," too, was greatly weakened. "The political signi-

ficance of the control of the Chinese Customs by the imperialists,"
a once widely-read historian in the People's Republic of China has
written with some venom and partial truth, "lay in the fact that they
used part of the spoils from the exploitation of the Chinese people
to support the Manchu regime which they hoped would serve as an
instrument to keep the people down."[1]   That the foreign treaty
powers, in support of their trade and other interests in China, preferred a stable status quo--whether a Manchu dynasty or an amenable
republican government--to sectarian rebellion, peasant uprisings, or
anti-imperialist mobilization--cannot be gainsaid.   Before 1894-95,
the overall effect of their numerous individual and joint actions was
to lend support to an ancien régime which itself still possessed the
political and psychological resources to rule.   By the turn of the
century, however, domestic political forces had been set in train--
Chinese nationalism, first in a conservative and then increasingly
in a revolutionary guise--which make it distinctly problematic that
the foreign presence in the Maritime Customs or the Salt Administration had more than a tertiary effect on the drama of twentieth-
century Chinese history.   Like the foreign establishment writ large,
these particular manifestations were gall to Chinese nationalists,
and in that sense affected the historical outcome.   But their specific
fiscal and political consequences were small, and not always clearly
in the interest of the stability the foreigners sought.

Maritime Customs.   Through 1900 the Customs Service was
under the jurisdiction of the Tsungli Yamen with which agency the
inspector-general (I. G.), whose office was located in Peking from 1865
onward, was in almost daily contact.   Transfer to the jurisdiction
of the Ministry of Foreign Affairs which replaced the Tsungli Yamen
in 1901 was uneventful.   But the establishment of a separate Revenue
Bureau (Shui-wu Ch'u) in July 1906--not at the ministry (pu) level,
although headed at first by T'ieh Liang, the minister of finance,
and T'ang Shao-yi, the vice-minister of foreign affairs--to supervise
the Customs Service was seen by foreign governments, customs staff,
and bondholders whose securities were linked to the customs revenue
as a threat to the special foreign character of the Service as it had
evolved over a half century.   Its organizational structure, its responsibilities and procedures, and the composition of its personnel as of
the first years of the twentieth century were largely the creation of
Robert Hart (1835-1911) who presided autocratically as inspector-
general of maritime customs from 1863 to 1908.[2]

In the course of fifty years in the service of China, Hart had accumulated a degree of personal power and independence that could not have been envisioned and certainly would not have been conceded by the Tsungli Yamen when he first took office. Far from doubting where his first loyalty lay, however, over the decades the I.G. had repeatedly emphasized to his foreign staff that they and he were employees of the Chinese government. No mere "imperialist" cynicism this: Hart and others like him--in an age when British commerce still dominated the sea-lanes of the world and made possible that combination of "civilizing mission" and squalid greed which led temporarily to European domination of Asia and Africa--genuinely believed that no conflict existed between the interests of a China potentially transformable into a "modern" state and those of the European powers, England in the lead, which would provide the models. He could write in 1885, with no tongue in cheek, declining the position of British minister to China:

> My disappearance at this moment from the Chinese Customs to occupy another post in China would affect the Customs Service most seriously, and so mischievously that the commercial interests which require an honest administration, and the international relations which look for improvement from the advancement of China, would by and by alike have reason to wish that the change had not taken place, whereas by remaining where I am, I believe I can make such a use of the insight into the future, afforded by the effect the news of my proposed retirement has already produced, as to give the Customs Service a broader foundation and a more durable status-- a result much to be desired, not only for the sake of the Service itself, but in the interests of British relations generally with China. . . .[3]

In 1906 Hart was seventy-one and in poor health; his retirement was imminent. To replace Hart with an equally powerful successor was out of the question in the decade of the Manchu reform movement--the conservative nationalist attempt in the aftermath of the defeat of Japan in 1894-1895, the reform movement of 1898, and the Boxer uprising of 1900 to refurbish the administration and ameliorate the international position of the Ch'ing empire. The perhaps gentler "imperialism of free trade" of the nineteenth century had given way to a fiercer international rivalry for the placement of loans to the

Chinese government, territorial concessions, the exploitation of railroads and mines, diplomatic influence in Peking, and "spheres of
influence" in the provinces. Between 1895 and 1898 the whole of the
then customs revenue had become pledged to the repayment of foreign
loans contracted to finance the costs of the war with Japan and the
large indemnity imposed by the Treaty of Shimonoseki, making the
Service in effect a debt-collecting agency for foreign bondholders.
Nationalist resentment was given further grounds for seeing the Customs Service as a tool of foreign interests when the unencumbered
balance of the Maritime Customs revenue and the collections of the
Native Customs within fifty li of the treaty ports--now placed under
the control of the foreign Inspectorate--were pledged for the service
of the Boxer Indemnity. The treaty powers were not timid in insis-
ting that the service of these foreign debts, as much as the inspec-
tion and taxation of imports and exports in facilitation of foreign
trade with China, was the raison d'être of the Service. Such was
the implication of the clauses, sanctioned by imperial edict, in the
loan agreements of 1896 and 1898 with the syndicate composed of the
Hongkong and Shanghai Banking Corporation and the Deutsch-Asiatische
Bank that during the currency of the loans the administration of the
Maritime Customs should remain as then constituted, and also of the
exchange of notes in 1898 by which Britain bound China to agree that
so long as British trade predominated the inspector-general would be
a British subject. The Customs, furthermore, administered the
national Post Office with foreign nationals in the key executive positions, managed the lighthouse service, controlled the pilotage in
China's harbors which in many ports was almost entirely in foreign
hands, and through its statistical, commercial, and cultural publications was for the foreign world China's sole official information
agency. And, after fifty years, no Chinese had yet been appointed
to a responsible administrative position--not even as an "assistant"
at any treaty port--within the Service.

The establishment of the Shui-wu Ch'u was a mild attempt, as
much as could be managed in the face of predictable foreign opposition, to downgrade somewhat the status of the Maritime Customs and
to ensure that Hart's successor would not amass the influence or
attain the independence that the circumstances of the Maritime Customs first half century had bestowed on "the I.G." Francis Aglen's
political role in Peking during his eighteen years as inspector-general,
in fact, never came near rivalling that of Hart. The new I.G. and
his foreign staff were much less centrally involved in China's inter-

national relations than had been the case in the nineteenth century.
Chinese began to appear in junior administrative positions in the
elite Indoor Staff after 1911. But little significant sinification of the
Customs occurred before the establishment of the Nanking government in 1928. Indeed, as will be noted below, foreign control over
the disposal of the revenue was increased as a consequence of the
Republican Revolution of 1911.

To all those who shared political power during the era of Yuan
Shih-k'ai's presidency and the various Peking governments which succeeded it, the existence of a foreign-controlled Customs Service was
one of the few constant and concrete manifestations of the unified and
centralized China which each thought he could reestablish under his
own aegis. It collected the revenues on foreign and coastal trade
with more than minimal probity. While before 1917 there was no
"Customs revenue surplus," in the sense of an available balance
after provision for loan service and the Boxer Indemnity which could
be released to the Peking government to use as it determined, the
prospect was that this amount would increase--to the potential benefit of whomever was in power in Peking. Efficient service of the
large foreign debt and the Indemnity helped keep the treaty powers
at bay, even if it did not importantly diminish their influence in
China. And when cancelled Indemnity obligations to Germany,
Austria, and Russia together with Customs revenue surpluses were
utilized to guarantee the domestic loans of the Peking government,
the fact that the service of these loans was to be in the hands of
the foreign inspector-general of Customs--who was seen by investors
as politically neutral among the contending Chinese factions--substan-
tially strengthened the government's credit.

The principal responsibilities of the Maritime Customs were,
of course, prevention of smuggling, examination of cargoes, and
assessment of the treaty tariff on imports, exports, and the coastal
trade. Its jurisdiction extended to "foreign-type vessels," whether
owned by foreigners or by Chinese, and to junks chartered by foreigners.[4] From the Treaty of Nanking in 1842 until recovery of
tariff autonomy in 1928-1930, the tariff for which the Customs was
responsible was subject to the agreement of all the treaty powers;
in effect it was imposed upon China by its trading partners. For
the most part a fixed schedule vaguely intended to yield approximately
5 percent ad valorem on both imports and exports, the tariff was
revised upward in 1858-1860, 1902, 1919, and in 1922 with the stated

purpose of achieving an effective ad valorem return of 5 percent on imports. The 1902 tariff, however, yielded only 3.2 percent and that of 1919 only 3.6 percent.[5] Foreign goods imported from abroad or from another Chinese treaty port (unless covered by an exemption certificate certifying that duty had been paid at the original port of entry) were assessed the full import duty. These goods could be carried inland exempt from likin taxation en route to their destination under a transit pass obtained from the Customs by payment of one-half of the stated import duty. Chinese goods exported abroad or to another Chinese treaty port were assessed the full export duty; if reshipped to a second Chinese port, they paid an additional coast trade duty equal to one-half the export duty. Chinese goods sent from the interior to a treaty port for shipment abroad under an outward transit pass which freed them from likin en route were charged transit dues by the Customs at one-half the rate of the export duty.[6] Customs offices at certain ports also collected wharfage dues (approximately 2 percent of the customs duty) and conservancy dues (3 percent of the customs duty). Tonnage dues (prorated to the displacement of the vessel) and measurement fees (depending on the tonnage) were levied at all ports. Tonnage dues were for the most part allocated for the maintenance of lighthouses and other navigation aids under Customs jurisdiction. Wharfage and conservancy dues were collections on behalf of various local and municipal authorities.

The Maritime Customs house at each treaty port was a Sino-foreign enterprise with jurisdiction shared by a Chinese superintendent (chien-tu) appointed by the Shui-wu Ch'u and a foreign commissioner appointed by the inspector-general. (Only the I.G. himself was a direct appointee of the Chinese government.) While sometimes deferring in form to the superintendent, in practice the commissioner was primus inter pares. The Indoor Staff (i.e., the executive function) at the port was solely under the commissioner's orders. It was the commissioner and not the superintendent who dealt with the foreign consuls when disputes with foreign traders arose. The superintendent, however, appointed his own recording staff (called shu-pan until 1912 and lu-shih thereafter) through whom he was to be kept informed on a daily basis of the revenue collections. Native Customs stations situated within a fifty-li radius of the port were administered by the commissioners and their revenue remitted for payment of the Indemnity, except that in matters of office staff and practice the commissioner was enjoined to act in conjunction with the superintendent. Native Customs stations outside

of the fifty-li radius were under the sole jurisdiction of the superintendent.

Before October 1911, the inspector-general and his commissioners did not actually collect, bank, and remit the Customs revenue
at the several treaty ports. The I.G., through the commissioners,
was responsible only for the correct assessment of the duties and
an accurate accounting to the Chinese government of the amounts
assessed. Foreign and Chinese traders paid their duties directly
into the authorized customs bank(s) (hai-kuan kuan-yin-hao), entirely
Chinese firms selected usually by the superintendents who were responsible to the imperial government for the security of the revenue
and whose accounts were checked against the returns submitted by
the foreign commissioners. In the wake of the Wuchang uprising in
October 1911 and the collapse of central authority in much of China,
including the departure of many of the Ch'ing-appointed superintendents who feared for their personal safety, this system was radically
altered. Fearing that the revolutionary leaders in the provinces
would withhold the Customs revenues which were pledged to the service of foreign loans and the Boxer Indemnity, the commissioners
at the ports in the provinces which had declared their independence
from Peking, acting in the interests of the treaty powers, assumed
direct control of the revenue and placed it in foreign banks. These
arrangements were perforce accepted by the republican government
which formally assumed power in February 1912, and were expressed
in an agreement imposed upon the Chinese government by the foreign
Diplomatic Body in Peking which 1) provided for the formation of an
International Commission of Bankers at Shanghai to superintend the
payment of the foreign loans of the Chinese government secured on
the Customs revenue and of the Boxer Indemnity; and 2) entrusted
the inspector-general with the collection of the revenue at the ports,
its remittance to Shanghai for deposit in the foreign custodian banks
"for account of the loans concerned and Indemnity payments," and
responsibility for making loan payments as they fell due according
to the priority determined by the Commission of Bankers.

Two implications of the 1912 agreement, which remained effective until the establishment of the Nanking government, should be
noted. The treaty powers until 1921 assumed the right to determine
whether or not there was a "Customs revenue surplus," after the
foreign debt was serviced, and to give their approval before the re-
lease of any funds to the Peking government. Their estimates of

the available surplus were conservative, to the ineffective displeasure
of successive administrations in Peking. Moreover, large sums of
Chinese government funds which formerly were at the disposal of
Chinese banks were now deposited in three foreign banks in Shanghai--
the Hongkong and Shanghai Banking Corporation, the Deutsch-
Asiatische Bank (until 1917 when China declared war on Germany),
and the Russo-Asiatic Bank (until its liquidation in 1926). While
interest was duly paid, large balances were always available to
these banks for their other commercial operations, and in the service of the foreign debt they profited substantially from handling
the necessary currency exchange operations.

While the conventional honesty of the Customs Service was
rarely questioned, it was not by contemporary international standards a particularly cost-efficient operation. The first charge on
the Customs revenue was the "office allowance" to cover the salaries and operating expenses of the Service. This allowance was
negotiated directly between the Chinese government and the inspector-
general, and in 1893 was set at Hk. Tls. (Haikwan taels) 3,168,000
per annum, a figure not increased until 1920 when the allowance
was raised to Hk. Tls. 5,700,000. In addition, the upkeep of the
superintendents' offices annually consumed approximately Hk. Tls.
400,000. Total revenue in 1898 was reported at Hk. Tls. 22,503,000
and in 1920 at Hk. Tls. 49,820,000. The cost of collection--not
including bankers' commissions and possible losses by exchange
incurred in collecting and remitting the net revenue--amounted therefore to 15.9 percent and 12.2 percent of the total revenue in these
two years. In 1898 the office allowance supported a staff of 895
foreigners and 4,223 Chinese (including 24 foreigners and 357 Chinese in the Postal Department) at an average cost of Hk. Tls. 619.
By 1920 the Customs staff numbered 1,228 foreigners and 6,246
Chinese (postal personnel were separated from the Customs in 1911),
reflecting the fact that many new ports had been opened to trade in
the intervening years. The 1920 increase, which brought the average cost to Hk. Tls. 763, compensated for the strain on the finances
of the Service occasioned by this expansion.

The Customs staff, Chinese and foreign, were assigned to one
of the three branches of the Service: the Revenue Department, the
Marine Department (established in 1865), and the Works Department
(established in 1912). Surveys of the coast and inland waterways,
the operation of lighthouses and lightships, the servicing of buoys

and beacons, and the maintenance and policing of harbors were the
responsibilities of the Marine Department. By 1911 it had established and was maintaining 132 lights, 56 lightships, 138 buoys
(many of which were whistling or gaslighted), and 257 beacons
(mainly on the Yangtze and West rivers). The Works Department
was charged with the erection and repair of Customs buildings and
property. But the heart of the Service, of course, was the Revenue
Department.

Within the Revenue Department were three classes of personnel:
Indoor, Outdoor, and Coast Staffs, each of which in turn was divided
into "foreign" and "native" sections. The Indoor Staff at each port
was the executive arm of the Customs responsible for administration
and accounting. It was headed by a commissioner who was assisted
by a deputy commissioner and four grades of assistants, all appointed,
promoted, assigned, and transferred by the inspector-general who
merely reported the appointments to the Shui-wu Ch'u. While Hart,
like Reverend Lobenstine quoted earlier who envisaged the creation
of a "Church . . . truly indigenous in China," repeated on more than
one occasion the intention expressed in a memorandum of 1864 to the
effect that the foreign Inspectorate "will have finished its work when
it shall have produced a native administration, as honest and as efficient to replace it,"[7] in fact no Chinese attained even the lowest
grade of assistant in the Indoor Staff during his tenure as I.G. He
had once thought that the Chinese linguist-clerks (t'ung-wen kung-shih),
who were required to have some knowledge of written and spoken
English, might eventually furnish recruits into the class of assistants.
Mainly graduates from mission schools, the Chinese education of
these clerks was probably deficient; in any case it was a lacuna repeatedly alleged to be an obstacle to their appointment to higher
official positions. Hart was also able to cite the opposition of higher
officials in Peking to the promotion of the clerks, which is perhaps
not surprising given their mission school background and their largely
south Chinese provenance. Many were Cantonese in origin, with the
next largest contingents coming from Kiangsu, Chekiang, and Fukien.
They were usually recruited by examinations held by the commissioners at the largest ports and, in addition to competence in English, were selected in part for their knowledge of several local dia-
lects. Originally mainly used as interpreters and translators, by
the time of Hart's death many were performing the same office
duties as the foreign assistants. The founding in 1908 of the Customs College (Shui-wu hsüeh-t'ang) eventually provided a pool of

well-trained graduates from whom, along with the most qualified of the clerks, Aglen (who could not completely ignore nationalist sentiment) began to appoint a number of Chinese assistants.

The shu-pan or lu-shih, the superintendent's accounting staff, have already been referred to. The third group of Chinese employees in the Indoor Staff were the writers and copyists, skilled in the use of documentary Chinese and calligraphy, who prepared all the official Chinese correspondence between the commissioner or superintendent and local officials, as well as the documents forwarded to the Inspectorate in Peking for transmission to the Shui-wu Ch'u.

In 1915 the personnel of the Indoor Staff of the Revenue Department, by position and nationality, were distributed as in Table 6.[8] The foreign Indoor Staff was recruited either through the Customs office in London, for the dominant British cohort, or through direct nomination to the I.G. by the several foreign legations in Peking. Many were young men with a university education who perhaps saw greater opportunities for themselves in China than appeared to be available in their home lands. There was some pressure on the Inspectorate to make these appointments in proportion to the size of each treaty power's trade with China, which accounts, for example, for the circumstance that there were no Japanese at all in 1895, sixteen--all assistants--in 1905, and thirty-seven--including two commissioners--in 1915. British predominance reflects the fact that through 1911 the percentage of the total Customs revenue accounted for by trade carried in British vessels never fell below 60 percent. Even in 1915, in the midst of World War I, British vessels carried 42 percent of the total value of China's foreign and interport trade cleared through the Customs.[9]

From the beginning of the Service, Hart emphasized the importance of a competent knowledge of spoken and written Chinese by the commissioners and assistants. Newly arrived appointees to the Indoor Staff were expected to undertake language study in Peking before being assigned to a port. A compulsory annual language examination for all foreign Indoor employees was ordered in 1884, and from 1899 in principle no one could be promoted to deputy commissioner or commissioner without an adequate knowledge of Chinese. Assistants who failed to qualify in the spoken language at the end of their third year in rank or in written Chinese at the end of the fifth year were, again in principle, to be discharged. But on this matter

TABLE 6

INDOOR STAFF OF THE REVENUE DEPARTMENT, 1915

	British	American	French	German	Russian	Other European	Japanese	Chinese	Total
Inspector-General	1	–	–	–	–	–	–	–	1
Commissioners	23	3	3	5	3	4	2	–	43
Deputy Commissioners	11	1	3	4	–	3	–	–	22
Assistants	76	11	4	17	10	37*	32	60	247
Miscellaneous	10	1	2	2	–	2	–	–	17
Medical Officers	31	5	5	2	–	3	3	9	58
Linguist Clerks	–	–	–	–	–	–	–	627	627
Chien-hsi**	–	–	–	–	–	–	–	33	33
Lu-shih	–	–	–	–	–	–	–	350	350
Writers and Copyists	–	–	–	–	–	–	–	110	110
Teachers	–	–	–	–	–	–	–	7	7
Shroffs	–	–	–	–	–	–	–	10	10
TOTAL	152	21	17	30	13	49	37	1,206	1,525
Total Non-Chinese	319								

* Includes one Korean.
**Graduates of Customs College, with provisional Customs ranks.

Hart was more generous than on many others in his treatment of his subordinates. The foreign Indoor Staff as a group was only moderately able in Chinese; many never got the hang of it; a few became distinguished sinologists. Aglen admonished the Service in October 1910: "The reports received this year on the Chinese acquirements of the In-door Staff, while showing that, on the whole, Chinese study is not altogether neglected, make it quite evident that the standard of efficiency throughout the Service is too low and that, with a few brilliant exceptions, study of Chinese is not taken seriously." The appearance of Chinese nationalism on the scene required something more. "It is more than ever necessary in these times, for the reputation of the Service and for its continued usefulness, that the reproach now beginning to be heard, that its members do not take sufficient interest in the country which employs them to learn its language should be removed. . . ."[10] Stricter examinations and classification of assistants by language ability were ordered immediately and outlined again in great detail in 1915. Aglen appeared satisfied with the results, but authentic competence in Chinese, among the Customs staff as among other foreigners, was achieved by very few.

The Outdoor Staff of the Revenue Department in 1915 comprised 881 foreigners and 3,352 Chinese. Except for 14 Chinese tidewaiters (checkers of cargo as it entered and left the port) out of a total of 490, all of the responsible positions--tidesurveyors and assistant tidesurveyors (the executives of the Outdoor Staff), boat officers, appraisers, chief examiners, assistant examiners, examiners, and tidewaiters--were filled by foreigners. Again British nationals dominated, accounting for 454 of the 881 foreigners and for 32 of the 57 top positions of tidesurveyor, assistant tidesurveyor, and boat officer. The remaining 3,238 Chinese were weighers, watchers, boatmen, guards, messengers, office coolies, gatekeepers, watchmen, and laborers. In the Coast Staff, also, the 40 commanders, officers, engineers, and gunners were all foreigners--29 of them British, while the 448 Chinese employees served as deck hands, engine hands, and cabin hands. A handful of Chinese out of the 1,239 employed in the Marine Department held "executive" posts, but these again were largely the preserve of the 117 foreigners. In the small Works Department, 14 of the 33 employees were Chinese. In sum, few of the 6,159 Chinese employees of the Customs, as compared with the 1,376 foreigners, were in other than menial positions.

Foreign members of the Outdoor Staff, unlike the Indoor Staff of the Revenue Department, were recruited locally in the several treaty ports. In the early years of the Service many were ex-sailors and adventurers who tried to make a go of it on the China coast. The distinction in social origin between the Indoor and Out-door Staffs continued into the twentieth century and was reflected in the much better treatment with respect to salaries, housing, allow-ances, and career opportunities enjoyed by the former who were recognized by other foreigners as part of the treaty port elite. As late as 1919, a deputation representing the foreign Outdoor Staff complained to Aglen about "the stigma attached to the word 'Out-door,' which extends beyond the Service and reacts on all social relations with the foreign community," and reported the "prevalent feeling . . that the In-door Staff goes out of its way to treat the Out-door Staff with contempt; that in disciplinary cases the Out-door Staff does not get a fair show, only one side of the case, and that the Commis-sioner's, being represented; . . . and that the private life of the Staff is unwarrantably interfered with by Tidesurveyors."[11]

The Customs Service, in fact, was seething with discontent by the time of Hart's departure, not only on the issue of elitism but as a general reaction to Hart's autocratic style. Aglen's official circu-lars as I. G. are hardly more modest in tone than those of his prede-cessor, but he did deal with some particular grievances, for example, establishing as of 1920 a supperannuation and retirement scheme, a move that Hart had long resisted.

In the last decade of the Ch'ing dynasty, total revenues from the Maritime Customs and from the Native Customs administered by the foreign Inspectorate came to about Hk. Tls. forty million per annum. Depending on how one estimates the total tax collections of the empire, a thorny subject upon which I cannot enter here, this represented 15 to 20 percent of all revenues, but a much higher proportion of those reported to and under the control of the central government--perhaps 25 to 40 percent. For the early years of the republic, fiscal data are, if anything, even more problematic. No reliable estimates of total tax collections have been made, while the proportion reported to and available for the use of the Peking government is uncertain except that--apart from the Customs revenue and the salt revenue until 1922--it grew ever less. What can be ascertained is that from 1912 through 1927, only about 20 percent of the total Maritime Customs revenue net of first charges was available to the Peking government for administrative and other expenditures.

While the payment of the Boxer Indemnity was formally secured on the Customs revenue, in practice before 1912 the funds remitted as monthly installments to the Foreign Bankers' Commission by the Shanghai taotai were not necessarily the Customs receipts which flowed from the Chinese customs banks to the Peking and provincial governments. The provinces were required to raise quotas totalling 18.8 million taels a year, which they met by increasing land and salt taxes, likin, and miscellaneous commercial levies, for the service of the Indemnity--to make up, it might be said, for the diversion of the Customs revenue. But only briefly after the 1911 revolution was the central government able to exert substantial control over the taxes, in particular the all-important land tax, collected by the provinces. Whence, then, came the Boxer payments? In fact now, and not just in name, from the receipts of the Maritime Customs and of the Native Customs administered by the Inspectorate. Loan service and Indemnity payments accounted for the remaining 80 percent of the net Customs revenue. These proportions, derived from the annual Customs accounts, are somewhat misleading inasmuch as cancelled (German, Austrian, and Russian from 1917) and deferred (Allied Powers between 1917 and 1922) Boxer installments, which in fact were hypothecated to service the Peking government's domestic borrowing, were nevertheless reported as Indemnity payments from the Customs revenue. The Customs surplus, too, when it became available, was utilized primarily as security for Peking's endless internal loans. As custodian of the several sinking fund accounts from which the service of these loans was to be met, the nonpolitical inspector-general provided an impartial administration generally satisfactory to all the factions which contended for power in Peking.

Because it was so closely linked to foreign trade and to the finances of the Chinese government--and in the nineteenth century with the central process of establishing a foreign presence in China, the Maritime Customs Service enjoyed an exceptional prominence within the foreign establishment. By the twentieth century, however, it had become a routinized organization, with little incremental effect on the bulk of the Chinese economy and only a niggardly contribution toward the training of its eventual Chinese successors. It survived in form under the Nationalist government, but only as a bit player in contrast to the leading roles of its younger years.

Post Office. In the first years of the Chinese republic, six of the treaty powers maintained post offices and independent postal services in China: Great Britain at twelve large cities and in three locations in Tibet; France in fifteen cities; Germany in sixteen cities; Japan at twenty cities in China proper, six locations in its "leased territory" in Manchuria, and twenty-three elsewhere in Manchuria; Russia at twenty-eight places, including many in Manchuria and Mongolia; and the United States at Shanghai only. The invariable justification for these foreign post offices, which were clear violations of China's sovereignty in that they had no basis in the treaties which otherwise limited that sovereignty, was that "safety of communications in China was not assured."[12] Although China's adherence to the Universal Postal Union in 1914 rendered void the special provisions of the Règlement d'Exécution of the 1906 Universal Postal Convention which had given some international legal basis to the continuance of foreign post offices on Chinese territory, it was not until the Washington Conference of 1921-1922 that the treaty powers agreed to their abolition as of January 1923. This concession to China's nationalist feelings did not, however, come without some strings attached: offices in foreign "leased territories" (which the Japanese claimed to understand as including their "railway zones" in Manchuria) were to continue, and the status of the foreign postmaster-general in the Chinese postal administration was not to be changed.

The foreign post offices competed with the Chinese Post Office in the major ports where the potential postal traffic was more lucrative without having any responsibility to serve less profitable outlying areas. They were notoriously lax in enforcing Chinese customs regulations, and on several occasions after 1914 had refused to handle mails from Chinese offices intended for overseas addresses. A necessity, perhaps, in the 1860s when they first appeared, their continuance for any reason other than as a mark of the foreigner's special position in China had become redundant as China itself developed a modern postal system. This development had taken place under the aegis of the Maritime Customs.[13] From the Customs Post, which began in the 1860s as a service carrying the correspondence of the several foreign legations between Peking and the treaty ports, there evolved in the 1870s and 1880s a postal service operated on Western lines available to all users. It was not much competition for the native postal agencies (hsin-chü) or the foreign postal establishments in the treaty ports before it was formally transformed into the Imperial Post Office in March 1896, but it expanded steadily thereafter.

Under the new arrangement, the management of the Imperial
Post Office was vested in the inspector-general who operated it as
a department of the Customs Service. The commissioners at the
several ports were responsible also for the postal affairs of their
districts. In 1898, 24 foreigners and 357 Chinese were detached
from the Customs for service in the Postal Department. Making
good its claim to an official monopoly was accomplished in part by
regulating and restricting the activities of the hsin-chü, in part by
absorbing these native postal agencies. In 1906 specially designated
postal commissioners were assigned to Shanghai, Canton, and Hankow in order to relieve the more overburdened Customs commissioners of their dual responsibilities. While the service and personnel of the Post Office grew (to 99 foreign and 11,885 Chinese
employees in 1911), its revenues lagged somewhat behind. Until
its separation from the Customs, annual supplements from the
Customs revenue were required to keep the Postal Department afloat.

That separation came in May 1911 when the Imperial Post
Office was transferred to the jurisdiction of the Ministry of Posts
and Communications and its management conceded to T. Piry, the
former postal secretary of the Customs Service, who was now to
become postmaster-general. Piry, a Frenchman, had joined the
Customs Service in 1874, was appointed postal secretary in 1901,
and continued as postmaster-general until 1917. That he was a
French national, as was his successor Henri Picard-Destelan, reflected China's commitment to France in 1898, during the "scramble
for concessions," "to take account of the recommendations of the
French Government in respect to the selection of the Staff" of its
postal service. Piry's authority as postmaster-general, however,
was more circumscribed than that of the inspector-general of customs had been, inasmuch as he was formally subordinated to a
"director-general" (chü-chang) of the Ministry, in line with China's
growing nationalist sentiment. Although much more an authentic
department of the Chinese government after 1911 than was the Customs Service even under Aglen, many of the leading postal administrative positions in Peking and the provinces continued to be filled
by foreigners (transferred at first from the Customs) during the next
two decades. The typical pattern was to have a foreign commissioner head a postal district, seconded by Chinese or foreign deputy
commissioners and Chinese and foreign assistants. A foreign staff
of about twenty-five was attached to the postmaster-general's (offi-
cially he was styled "co-director-general") office in Peking, and

about seventy-five other foreigners were stationed in the provinces.
In 1920, about half of the foreigners were British nationals, one-
quarter French, and the rest scattered among a dozen other nationalities. Some thirty thousand Chinese employees actually processed
and delivered the mails.

Salt Administration. Imposed upon China in the twentieth century and not in the middle of the nineteenth, the Sino-foreign Inspectorate of Salt Revenues was something different from--and less than--
the Maritime Customs Service.

Chinese opposition to foreign participation in the Salt Administration, except in limited advisory and technical roles, stalled comple-
tion of negotiations for the Ł25,000,000 Reorganization Loan to Yuan
Shih-k'ai's new government from February 1912 until April 1913.
The principal treaty powers--England, France, Russia, Germany,
Japan, and the United States (which withdrew from the consortium
before the loan was concluded)--through the sextuple banking consortium sought to strengthen Yuan's government with the hope that it
would be able to maintain China's unity and protect foreign interests.
But the bankers would undertake a loan as large as Ł25,000,000 only
upon adequate security. The Customs revenue, completely hypothecated for the service of previous loans and the Indemnity, for an
undetermined time could be only a secondary guarantee; the Peking
government therefore pledged the proceeds of the salt revenue. As
a central condition for floating the loan, the consortium insisted
upon a measure of control over the Salt Administration, not merely
advice and audit, which the powers forced the increasingly bankrupt
Yuan to accept. Accordingly Article V of the April 26, 1913
Reorganization Loan agreement provided for the establishment, under
the Ministry of Finance, of a "Central Salt Administration" to comp-
prise a "Chief Inspectorate of Salt Revenues under a Chinese Chief
Inspector and a foreign Associate Chief Inspector." In each salt-
producing district there was to be a branch office "under one Chinese and one foreign District Inspector who shall be jointly responsible for the collection and the deposit of the salt revenues."

Patriotic sentiment was correct in seeing the insertion of an
explicit foreign interest into the administration of China's salt
revenues as a derogation of sovereignty, and the juxtaposition of
Chinese and foreign district inspectors in the provinces looked very
much like the Customs arrangement in which foreign commissioners

and Chinese superintendents nominally shared power at the treaty
ports. Perhaps, too, because the Salt Administration was a more
intimate part of the Chinese polity, one with delicate internal balances and long-standing interests, any foreign role at all was especially galling. The Salt Inspectorate, however, unlike the Customs
organization which was a new creation expanding in tandem with the
growth of foreign trade, represented at first only the interpolation
of a new echelon of administration into a perennial Chinese fiscal
complex comprising the manufacture, transportation, taxation, and
sale of salt. Superimposed upon these traditional arrangements to
insure that the revenues collected were in fact made available to
the central government for service of the Reorganization Loan, the
Inspectorate over time did acquire substantial de facto control over
salt manufacture and marketing. But this control was not linked to
any continuing and specifically foreign interest comparable to the
growth and protection of international commerce--apart from meeting
the installments of principal and interest set forth in the amortization table of the Reorganization Loan. The benefits, such as they
were, accrued mainly to whomever was in control of the Peking
government, and after 1922 mainly to the provincial satraps.

The associate chief inspector and his foreign subordinates,
because they were representatives of the bankers of Europe, backed
in turn by their respective governments, of course were more than
the mere coadjutors that might be implied by a literal reading of
Article V. But no imperium in imperio resulted such as Robert
Hart erected for the Customs Service. Maximum foreign influence
was exercised in the very first years of the Inspectorate, when Yuan
Shih-k'ai's centralization efforts looked as if they had some promise
and the President gave his backing to Richard Dane, the first associate chief inspector. Dane (1854-1940), a former Indian civil ser-
vant who had served in turn as commissioner of salt revenue for
northern India and then as the first inspector-general of excise and
salt for India, was responsible for some far-reaching reforms of
the whole salt gabelle during his tenure in China from 1913 to 1917,
but he was never a Hart.[14] The minister of finance and the Chinese
chief inspector were not mere figureheads giving pro forma approval
to whatever Dane might undertake, but on the contrary themselves
represented a nationalist, albeit conservative, political current of
bureaucratic centralization whose interests for a time paralleled
those of the foreign syndicate and which gladly made use of such
pressure against local, centrifugal forces as a foreign presence
might provide.

There were, moreover, never more than 40 to 50 foreign employees of the Salt Administration (41 in 1917, 59 in 1922, and 41
in 1925 when Chinese employees totalled 5,363) while more than
1,300 served in the Maritime Customs in the early republic.[15]   The
large Chinese staff, in contrast to the Customs Service, was not
under the control of the foreign chief inspector.   Perhaps a dozen
foreigners provided the administrative staff of the foreign chief
inspector in Peking, while the remainder were stationed in the several salt districts as auditors, district inspectors, assistant district
inspectors, or assistants.   Because what they, and their Chinese
colleagues who occupied parallel ranks, were inspecting and auditing
was not a foreign trade but a major component of China's domestic
commerce and fiscal system, the Chinese colleagues could hardly be
relegated to the largely supernumerary status of the Customs superintendents.   The foreign staff, as opposed to Chinese agents of a
Salt Administration reformed with foreign assistance, did not pene-
trate to the base of the labyrinthian salt complex.   In the case of
the Maritime Customs, the foreigner was simultaneously the principal
participant in the activity that was being regulated and taxed, the
effective regulator and collector, and before 1928 the final recipient
in the form of loan and Indemnity payments of the bulk of the revenue.
But the specific foreign interest in the Salt Administration extended
only to insuring that the revenues were paid on time to the foreign
consortium banks.   From July 1917, by which time the Customs
revenue had grown to the point that it was able to carry the service
of the Reorganization Loan as well as all previous foreign obligations
directly charged on it, repayment of the Reorganization Loan was
only indirectly linked to a foreign presence in the Salt Administration.

To be sure British influence in Peking and in the Yangtze valley
was enhanced by the facts that the associate chief inspector was a
British national and that almost half of the foreign staff were also
British.   (The Japanese were the second most numerous foreigners
in the Salt Inspectorate.)   The control exercised by the two chief
inspectors over the "salt surplus," i.e., collections in excess of
the installments due on the Reorganization Loan, which was based
upon provisions of the loan agreement requiring that the salt revenue
be deposited in the foreign banks gross without any deduction and
"be drawn upon only under the joint signatures of the Chief Inspectors," moreover, gave Dane great leverage in Peking.   That leverage was meaningful, however, only so long as provincial authorities
and military commanders continued to remit substantial salt revenues

to Peking.   After 1922 both the total reported collections and the
proportion received by the central government fell precipitously.
While the Customs revenues remained centralized, even at the height
of the warlord era, the Sino-foreign Inspectorate could not and did
not attempt to prevent the provinces from sequestering the salt
revenue.   Dane's successors--Reginald Gamble, also a former commissioner of salt revenue for northern India, from 1918; and E. C. C.
Wilton, a former British diplomat with long service in China, from
1923--inevitably enjoyed much less influence than Dane did.   The
placement of a Russian national, R. A. Konovaloff, formerly of the
Customs Service, in charge of the audit department supervising the
expenditure of the Reorganization Loan, and of a German, C. Rump,
at the head of a loan department concerned with future Chinese government borrowing--all parts of the squabbling for influence among
the treaty powers during the loan negotiations in 1913--likewise
produced little benefit to either government.   Konovaloff was told
only what the Chinese wanted him to know, and Rump was never
consulted.

V. ECONOMIC INTERESTS

The foreign economic presence in China in the early twentieth century was a very visible one, but that conspicuousness itself constitutes something of a paradox. Foreign firms, investments, loans, and personnel dominated important parts of the modern sector of China's economy in the early republic. The modern sector, however, although it is prominently recorded both in contemporary sources and retrospective studies, represented only a minute portion of the Chinese economy as a whole. Neither foreign nor Chinese modern enterprise, while both grew steadily, bulked very large before 1949. As late as 1933, 63 to 65 percent of gross domestic product originated in agriculture, for the most part organized and operated along traditional lines and entirely without direct foreign participation. The South Manchurian Railway Company operated a number of experimental farms in Manchuria, but in no part of China were there foreign-owned plantations producing even the major agricultural export items (tea, silk, vegetable oil and oil products, egg products, hides and skins, and bristles) not to speak of the rice, wheat, vegetables, and cotton which were China's main crops. Handicraft production, again with no foreign participation, accounted for 7 percent of GDP in 1933 compared to 2.2 percent for modern industry in which the foreign share was significant. Transportation by junk, cart, animal, and human carriers was three times as important (4 percent of GDP) as the modern transportation sector in which foreign-owned or operated railroads and foreign steamships appeared so prominently. China's foreign trade and even her interport trade were carried mainly in foreign vessels, but total foreign trade turnover certainly never exceeded (and probably never reached) 10 percent of gross domestic product. If all foreign owned, controlled, operated, or influenced enterprises could, hypothetically, have been nationalized in 1915, and all public and private indebtedness to foreign creditors cancelled, the overall effect in yielding a "surplus" that could, again hypothetically, have been used for economic and social development would have been as nothing compared to the potential surplus of 37 percent of net domestic product calculated by Carl Riskin as becoming available as a consequence of the redistribution of wealth and income after 1949.[1]

But the foreign businessman and alien capital were nevertheless present in early republican China. What forms did they assume and

what influence did they have?[2]   I shall look in turn at trade, banking,
manufacture and mining, transportation, and public finance.

Trade.   Foreign firms listed in the annual North-China Desk
Hong List published by the North-China Daily News & Herald, Limited
in Shanghai, or in The Directory & Chronicle for China, Japan,
Corea . . . issued by the Hongkong Daily Press Office ranged from
such giants as Jardine, Matheson and Company and Carlowitz and Company to the modest Sweetmeat Castle, "pastry cooks, confectioners,
bakers, wine and spirit merchants" or the Schlacterei W. Fütterer,
butcher to the German community in Shanghai. By trade they encom-
passed among others, accountants, advertising agents, banks, brokers,
commission merchants and agents, engineers, general merchants, lawyers, outfitters, physicians and dentists, printers and publishers,
shipowners and shipping agents, undertakers, and wine and spirit
merchants.   Many were retail establishments or services catering
exclusively to the foreign residents of the treaty ports.   Some were
manufacturers who operated plants in China.   The largest and most
typical, however, engaged in importing or exporting or in some service ancillary to foreign trade, with which manufacturing operations
were sometimes combined.

Their number varied somewhat from year to year.   On the
margin, for the smaller firms at least, failures occurred, while the
total increased along with the expansion of trade.   I earlier cited
Customs estimates that the number of foreign "firms," head offices,
and branches counted separately, in the treaty ports in 1918 was
nearly 7,000.   Typically, excluding Japanese and Russian firms in
Manchuria, the head offices in China of the larger enterprises were
located in either Shanghai or Hong Kong, with varying numbers of
branches maintained at other ports.   (The home office in Europe or
Japan in many cases also directed operations in other parts of Asia.)
One additional respect in which the Customs data given in Table 1
are defective is that they do not reflect the trend toward a stagnation
or decline in the number of branches in the "outports" in relation to
the number of head offices in Shanghai or Hong Kong which the his-
tories of individual firms and an analysis of the structure of China's
foreign trade strongly suggest.   The resident foreign merchant played
a critical role in the import-export trade, but in the early republic
his function had for some time been largely restricted to that point
in the commercial process at which foreign goods were landed in
China or Chinese goods loaded on ship for export abroad.   There

were exceptions to be sure, and they will be noted below, but as I
have argued elsewhere, "It is perhaps only a small exaggeration,
with respect to the importation and distribution of the major staples
of commerce, to describe the foreign trading firms in China as
having been gradually transformed into Shanghai and Hong Kong
commission agents serving the established Chinese commercial network. "3

Jardine, Matheson and Company, whose origins antedated the
Opium War, and Butterfield and Swire, which commenced business
in Shanghai in 1867, were the most prominent of the British trading
firms in China in the early twentieth century.   Unlike many of the
"grand old China houses, " both survived the radical changes in China
trade of the 1870s and 1880s when to a major extent the merchant
importing for the market on his own account was displaced by the
"commission merchant. "   Jardine's head office for China was in
Hong Kong, and it had branches in every major port.   In addition to
its general foreign trade department and numerous agencies, the
firm controlled the Indo-China Steam Navigation Company (whose
forty-one steamers were a major presence on the Yangtze) and the
large Shanghai and Hongkew Wharf Company; operated a major cotton
mill (Ewo) and a silk filature in Shanghai; represented the Russian
Bank for Foreign Trade and the Mercantile Bank of India, as well
as numerous marine and fire insurance companies and several shipping lines; and had close ties with the Hongkong and Shanghai Banking
Corporation.   Butterfield was somewhat smaller, but in addition to
its Shanghai headquarters maintained branches at Canton, Swatow,
Amoy, Foochow, Ningpo, Chinkiang, Nanking, Wuhu, Kiukiang, Hankow, Ichang, Chefoo, Tientsin, and Newchwang.   It operated the
China Navigation Company, with a fleet of more than sixty steamers
on the Yangtze and along the coast; managed the Taikoo Sugar Refining
Company and the Taikoo Dockyard and Engineering Company in Hong
Kong; and had numerous shipping and insurance agencies.   (I note
here that more than two hundred European insurance companies were
represented by Shanghai firms before World War I.)   Gibb, Living-
ston and Company was also an old British firm in China and earlier
had had branches in Canton, Foochow, Tientsin, and at various Yangtze ports.   In the second decade of the twentieth century, however,
it maintained offices only in Shanghai, Hong Kong, and Foochow.
Gibb devoted itself to the exportation of tea and silk, general commission business for which it had many agencies, Shanghai real es-
tate, and shipping and insurance agencies--the list is familiar by now.

Founded in 1875, Ilbert and Company was one of the first British trading firms to operate exclusively as a "commission merchant," importing goods which were bought on indent terms by Chinese merchants. It also operated the Laou Kung Mao Spinning and Weaving Company in Shanghai. One could go on--Dodwell and Company, tea exports and cotton piece good imports, shipping and insurance agencies, for example, and others--but the increasing German and Japanese competition which the British traders faced in the early republic should also be noted.

Siemssen and Company, established in Shanghai in 1856, was the oldest German house in Shanghai and maintained offices also in Hong Kong, Canton, Hankow, Tientsin, and Tsingtao. The firm was best known as engineers and contractors of complete equipment for factories and railroads, for its insurance agencies, as well as its extensive import-export business. Carlowitz and Company, which had commenced business in China in the 1840s, was perhaps the largest German firm. Shipping agents, managers of the Yangtze Wharf and Godown Company at Shanghai, exporters of wool, straw-braids, egg products, and bristles--Carlowitz was especially prominent as the importer of German heavy machinery, railroad and mining equipment (for the Han-Yeh-P'ing Iron and Steel Company and its P'ing-hsiang mines, for example), and weapons (as the exclusive agents in China for the Krupp works). Its main office in Shanghai in Kiukiang Road was the largest building in the International Settlement in 1908. Branches were located in Hong Kong, Canton, Tientsin, Hankow, Wuchang, Tsingtao, and Tsinanfu. A third important German trading firm, Melchers and Company, began business in Hong Kong in 1866 and opened its Shanghai office in 1877. Other branches were at Hankow, Canton, Tientsin, Swatow, Chinkiang, and Ichang. Melchers was the China agent for Norddeutscher Lloyd, and operated river steamers on the Yangtze and the Chang Kah Pang Wharf Company in Shanghai. The firm specialized in the exportation of hides and skins, bristles, silk, egg products, and vegetable oils. As an importer it handled European, British, and American machinery, and British textiles.

The China branches of Mitsui Bussan Kaisha, the largest Japanese trading company, were located at Shanghai, Amoy, Hong Kong, Foochow, Canton, Hankow, Tsingtao, Chefoo, Tientsin, Dairen, and Newchwang. In addition to representing leading Japanese manufacturers and insurance companies, Mitsui held agencies for several

well-known British, European, and American firms. It operated its
own steamer line, and owned and managed two spinning mills (Shanghai Cotton Spinning Company and Santai Cotton Spinning Company) in
Shanghai.

In the export trade, foreign merchants had earlier been importantly involved in establishing collecting organizations to obtain supplies from the scattered small producers and in making provisions
for the grading, sorting, and preliminary processing of materials
for export. Except for some processing operations (egg products,
hides, and brick tea by Russian merchants, for example), most of
these functions had been taken over by Chinese merchants by the
late nineteenth century. In the case of tea, the foreign trader almost
always bought in bulk from Chinese dealers at the ports. And although introduced by Europeans, the majority of modern silk filatures
by the beginning of the twentieth century were Chinese owned (sometimes with European, usually Italian, managers). The role of the
Chinese merchant in the import trade, once the goods had been
landed at a treaty port, was even more prominent. With the development of steam shipping from the 1860s, Chinese dealers in imported
cotton textiles or opium, for example, tended to bypass the smaller
ports and to purchase directly in Shanghai and Hong Kong. While
the foreign houses were not ousted from the smaller ports, some
branches were closed, and those that remained concentrated on the
collection of export goods and the sale of more specialized imports
rather than the distribution of staples which was largely in Chinese
hands. As a consequence of these developments, the business of the
foreign trading firms in the early republic had become heavily concentrated in the major treaty ports--in the actual importation (typically as a commission agent) of foreign goods for sale to Chinese
dealers at these ports, and in the exportation of Chinese goods (with
some processing) from these same places.[4]

Exceptions to the pattern of trade sketched above in the early
twentieth century were more likely to be the result of the initiatives
of German or Japanese firms than of the well-entrenched British
merchants. For certain types of goods, German munitions and dye-
stuffs at first, extensive distribution networks of Chinese agents
supervised by European inspectors and more direct methods of trading
were adopted upon the insistence and with the support of the home
manufacturers. Direct distribution through local Chinese agents who
worked on a commission basis was successful mainly with standardized

or proprietary goods such as cigarettes, kerosene, dyes, patent medicines, alkalis, and soap, although the Japanese organized part of their textile sales in this manner as well. In the sale of kerosene and of cigarettes--and in the manufacture of the latter in China as well--British and American firms other than the large commission merchants in the treaty ports took the lead.

The Standard Oil Company of New York shipped its first kerosene to China in the 1880s where it was sold by firms such as Butterfield and Jardine. In 1894, after the failure of lengthy negotiations with Jardine, Matheson and Company to have that firm become Standard's permanent sales agent in Asia, including China, Standard Oil undertook to establish its own marketing organization. At first it sold its kerosene only at Shanghai to Chinese dealers who handled all the "up-country" distribution. Standard Oil resident managers were, however, soon established in the major ports where bulk storage facilities were erected, who appointed and bonded Chinese "consignees" and closely supervised the sales of these agents and their numerous subagents. "In some places, as in Wuhu, for example, the hand of the New York company extended into street peddling."5 Specially prepared Chinese-language pamphlets and posters advertised Standard's premium "Devoe" brand and the cheaper "Eagle." The free distribution or sale at a very low price of small tin lamps with glass chimneys (the famous "Mei-foo" lamp) created a market for kerosene. By 1910 Standard Oil was shipping 15 percent of its total exports of kerosene to China. (A 1935 rural survey found that 54 percent of farm families regularly purchased kerosene.) American salesmen, many with college degrees, who came to China under three-year agreements providing passage home at the end of that period and the possibility of renewal, and Chinese assistants trained in American methods replaced the usual compradore staff of the foreign trading firm. Travelling constantly in the interior, required to learn the Chinese language, responsible for selecting dealers and insuring supplies in large territories, in perpetual conflict with Chinese officials over local taxes, Standard's agents penetrated into Chinese society as deeply as some of the more enterprising missionaries. Few foreign careers in China were as colorful as that of Roy S. Anderson, son of the missionary president of Soochow University in Shanghai and manager of Standard Oil's Chinkiang office, who participated actively on the republican side in the siege of Nanking in 1911 and in later years was the trusted go-between of warlords.

Standard Oil's chief competitor in China, the Asiatic Petroleum Company (a subsidiary of Royal Dutch Shell, an Anglo-Dutch alliance), operated through a similar sales network under its direct control. In spite of such departures from the usual pattern of trade as sending Western salesmen into the interior, erecting storage facilities in many Chinese cities, and maintaining ownership of the kerosene wherever it was transported until the actual retail sale, Standard Oil's and Asiatic Petroleum's success ultimately depended upon utilizing rather than replacing China's existing commercial system. Their Chinese "consignees," i.e., wholesalers or jobbers, were more often than not established merchants who had other commercial interests as well. Even the retail proprietors of Standard Oil's distinctive yellow-fronted shops were usually prominent local dealers. The foreigner's marketing structure was after all a superficial one, like that of the enterprising missionaries with whom I have compared their Western agents.

This dependence upon China's traditional marketing structure to reach the final consumer characterized as well the Singer Sewing Machine Company, Imperial Chemical Industries which sold chemicals based on alkalis, dyes, and fertilizer, and the enormously successful British-American Tobacco Company.[6] BAT was distinctive in that, in addition to importing cigarettes manufactured in England and America, it operated a half-dozen substantial factories of its own in China by 1915, which escaped significant direct taxation because of their claimed extraterritorial status. From 1913 BAT was actively involved in promoting the cultivation of tobacco grown from American seeds by Chinese peasants in Shantung--a foreign intrusion into agricultural production which was as rare in China as it was typical in the fully colonized Asian countries. But its system of distributors and dealers directed by a network of foreign agents was merely superimposed upon existing Chinese transportation and local marketing facilities. And in the distribution of seed and fertilizer in Shantung-- long a tobacco-growing area--as well as in its purchase of the crop, BAT relied primarily upon Chinese intermediaries. The direct foreign role was a more modest one than the company's public pronouncements claimed.

Beyond the commercial structure itself, what fundamentally limited the impact of foreign merchants and their goods--the large sales of kerosene, cigarettes, and of imported cotton piece goods before these last were ousted by the competition of cloth woven in

China were important exceptions of course--was the overall poverty
of the Chinese economy. Much has been written about the "myth"
of the China market which called many to Shanghai and the other
treaty ports, and I shall not repeat it here. Notwithstanding the
steady growth of both imports and exports after 1900, even in 1936
the per capita value of China's foreign trade, including Manchuria,
was still smaller than that of any other country. If, as some ana-
lysts suggest, neither China's share of world trade nor its per
capita foreign trade were "abnormally" low for an underdeveloped
country of its size and resource endowment, it is still true that
foreign demand for China's agricultural and mining exports generated
only very weak "backward linkages" (i. e., induced demand for the
production of other products in the Chinese economy), while the
imported manufactured or processed commodities went mainly to
satisfy final demand and consequently generated only weak "forward
linkages" (i. e., capital or raw material inputs into Chinese production). The hope of economic gain had brought the foreigner to
China, but it was less his specific economic influence than the political and psychological facts of his presence under privileged conditions
that directly affected the course of China's modern history.

Banking. In the absence of modern financial institutions in
China, the foreign merchant houses undertook to provide for themselves many of the auxiliary services such as banking, foreign
exchange, and insurance essential to their import-export business.
In time these subsidiary enterprises were replaced or supplemented
by newly established specialized firms. The first Western bank in
China, the Chartered Bank of India, Australia, and China which
opened a Shanghai branch in 1858, was still largely an appendage of
the Indian trade. Only with the organization of the Hongkong and
Shanghai Banking Corporation in 1864 did the China traders acquire
a locally controlled organ designed to meet their particular needs.
Although its directorate was a cosmopolitan body, the Hongkong
Bank was effectively a British institution. It began operations simultaneously in Hong Kong and Shanghai, and before the 1890s had few
serious competitors. By the second decade of the twentieth century,
twelve foreign banks were operating in China: Chartered Bank (head
office: London, branches: Canton, Foochow, Hankow, Hong Kong,
Shanghai, Tientsin); Hongkong and Shanghai Banking Corporation (head
office: Hong Kong, branches: Amoy, Canton, Foochow, Hankow,
Peking, Shanghai, Tientsin); Mercantile Bank of India (head office:
London, branches: Hong Kong, Shanghai); Banque de l'Indo-Chine,

in China from 1899 (head office: Paris, branches: Canton, Hankow, Hong Kong, Peking, Shanghai, Tientsin); Banque Sino-Belge, from 1902 (head office: Brussels, branches: Shanghai, Tientsin); Deutsch-Asiatische Bank, in China from 1889 (head office: Berlin, branches: Hankow, Hong Kong, Peking, Shanghai, Tientsin, Tsinanfu, Tsingtao); International Banking Corporation, from 1902 (head office: New York, branches: Canton, Hankow, Hong Kong, Peking, Shanghai); Nederlandsche Handel-Maatschappij, from 1903 (head office: Amsterdam, branches: Hong Kong, Shanghai); Russo-Asiatic Bank, from 1895 (head office: St. Petersburg, branches: Chefoo, Changchung, Hankow, Harbin, Hong Kong, Hulun, Kashgar, Kuldja, Newchwang, Peking, Shanghai, Tientsin, Tsitsihar); Yokohama Specie Bank, from 1893 (head office: Yokohama, branches: Antung, Changchun, Dairen, Hankow, Hong Kong, Liaoyang, Mukden, Newchwang, Peking, Port Arthur, Tiehling, Tientsin); and Bank of Taiwan (head office: Taipei, branches: Amoy, Canton, Foochow, Hong Kong, Shanghai, Swatow).

The majority of these banks engaged principally in financing the import and export trade of foreign firms. Some direct advances were also made to Chinese merchants, but their chief impact on the Chinese commercial structure took the form of short-term "chop loans" to the native banks (ch'ien-chuang) who in turn lent to Chinese merchants. These credits to the ch'ien-chuang, which ceased with the Revolution of 1911, for a time gave the foreign banks considerable leverage over the entire money market in Shanghai.[7] As they monopolized the financing of foreign trade, the banks in practice controlled the foreign exchange market in China. Fluctuations in the exchange rate between Chinese silver currency and gold which was the world standard were frequently large. The conduct of foreign exchange dealings and international arbitrage provided substantial profits to the foreign banks and in particular to the Hongkong Bank whose daily exchange rates were accepted as official rates by the entire Shanghai market. Their extraterritorial position was utilized by the foreign banks to issue bank notes, a right which the Chinese government never conceded but was powerless to counteract. The total value of foreign notes in circulation in 1916 nearly equalled the note issue of Chinese public and private banks combined.[8] Wealthy Chinese in particular preferred to deposit their liquid assets in foreign banks which enjoyed extraterritorial rights, one source of the steady silver income upon which the banks based their foreign exchange business. A more important source, however, resulted from the banks' role in servicing China's foreign debt and indemnity

payments which brought an endless inflow of customs and salt receipts
and of the working capital of many of the railroads. The major
banks, moreover, were directly involved in the placement of indemnity and railroad loans with European lenders which itself produced
large profits. Foreign companies holding railroad and mining concessions in China were frequently affiliates of the banks; the British
and Chinese Corporation was closely linked to the Hongkong Bank,
for example, as were the German Shantung railroad and mining companies to the Deutsch-Asiatische Bank. One study of British bankers'
profits in China from the issuance and service of foreign loans con-
cludes that they averaged from 4.5 percent (for nonrailroad loans)
to 11 percent (for railroad loans which normally included provisions
for profit-sharing and for the bank to act as a purchasing agent) of
the par value of the loans made in the years 1895-1914.[9]

While the foreign banks lost some of their privileged position
to the government-backed triumvirate of the Central Bank of China,
the Bank of China, and the Bank of Communications in the 1920s
and especially after the establishment of the Kuomintang regime,
they continued to be preeminent in the financing of foreign trade.
At any time, however, their influence on the Chinese economy outside of the foreign trade and government finance sectors was negli-
gible. Like the traders who were their chief customers, the foreign
banks affected China most because they were foreign, privileged, and
frequently arrogant.

There were, of course, some links with important political
consequences between foreign commercial and financial enterprise
and China's small but widespread modernizing sector. Speculation
in the Shanghai rubber market in 1910, for example, severely dam-
aged the Szechwan Railway Company, and its demands that these
losses be covered by the Peking government's scheme to nationalize
the Canton-Hankow Railroad and its branches helped precipitate the
1911 revolution. But, overall, while exchange fluctuations or financial panics in Shanghai might make headlines, Shanghai and the other
ports were only loosely tied to the economy of the vast hinterland.
Domination of the modern sector, if it could be achieved by outsiders--
or even by insiders--hardly constituted control of China as a whole
as subsequent history was to show.

Manufacture and Mining. I have described the number, nationality, location, and size of foreign-owned manufacturing and mining

enterprises in China as of 1913 in <u>The Chinese Economy, ca. 1870-1911</u> (1969). It may suffice here to note the dominant foreign share in the second decade of the twentieth century in four industries which together accounted for 52 percent of net value added by modern industry in 1933: cotton yarn and cloth (17.2 percent), cigarettes (4.0 percent), coal mining (13.4 percent), and electric power (17.4 percent).[10] Estimates are given in Table 7 for the size of the foreign share in coal mining and cotton textiles. In 1933 foreign-owned firms produced 35 percent of the total value of production by manufacturing industries as a whole, but no comparable overall estimate can be made for 1910-1920, at a time when 75 to 90 percent of modern coal mining and nearly half of the cotton textile industry were in foreign hands. Production figures are not available, but the cigarette industry was dominated by foreigners too, judging by a comparison of BAT's sales of twelve billion cigarettes in 1919 (a large part manufactured in China) with the two billion sold by its chief Chinese competitor, the Nanyang Brothers Tobacco Company. And the generation of electric power in the major ports--again no output data are available for 1910-1920--was also largely a foreign preserve.

Yet the caveats that I have already raised against reading large conclusions into statistics about the modern sector, just because they are the only quantitative data available, need to be faced once more. Cigarette sales certainly boomed after BAT was launched in 1902, but there is little evidence that the predominant forms in which tobacco was consumed outside of urban areas did not continue to be in the peasant's long pipe, in water pipes, or as snuff--all of which had been widespread since the seventeenth century. Even as late as 1935, only 19 percent of farm families purchased tobacco of any kind. In the case of cotton yarn, only 18 percent of total consumption in 1905, and 34 percent in 1919, was produced in modern mills, Chinese- and foreign-owned, in China. The comparable figures for cotton cloth are 1 percent and 5 percent in 1905 and 1919 respectively. Handicraft production and imports together accounted for 82 percent of the yarn consumed in 1905 and 66 percent in 1919; and for 99 percent and 95 percent of the cloth. These proportions suggest that China's most developed modern industry, cotton textiles, in which the foreign share loomed so large, did not clothe a substantial majority of the Chinese population. The average annual production during the years 1912-1921 of ten million tons of coal by modern mining methods--or even the annual total of sixteen million

TABLE 7

FOREIGN SHARES IN COAL MINING AND COTTON TEXTILE INDUSTRIES

	Coal Mining		Cotton Yarn and Cloth			
	Percent total output (tons) mined by modern methods from		Percent spindles and looms in operation*			
			Spindles		Looms	
	Foreign-owned mines	Sino-foreign mines	Foreign-owned	Chinese-owned	Foreign-owned	Chinese-owned
1910	----	----	30.3	69.7	----	100.0
1912	42.6	49.3	----	----	----	----
1914	----	----	46.0	54.0	50.1	49.9
1915	35.2	54.5	----	----	----	----
1918	34.1	43.2	----	----	----	----
1919	----	----	43.6	56.4	----	----
1920	----	----	41.9	58.1	49.0	51.0
1921	30.9	45.0	----	----	----	----

* Spindles and looms in Sino-foreign mills are allocated equally to foreign and Chinese ownership.

tons by modern and traditional mines together--provided only a meager proportion of the total energy consumed by the 450-500 million Chinese who, as in the past, continued to depend upon wood, straw, and vegetable wastes for their fuel. Even in 1933, China's total output of coal was only 28 million tons (compare 1973: 250 million metric tons), almost entirely consumed in the large cities, by railroads and steamers, and by the small modern manufacturing sector. Similarly, the 1.42 billion kilowatt hours of electricity produced in 1933 (compare 1973: 101 billion), of which 63 percent was accounted for by foreign-owned utilities, served exclusively the larger cities.

Of the forty-five cotton mills in China in 1919, fifteen were Japanese- and British-owned. On the average, the foreign mills spun yarn five to seven counts higher than the Chinese-owned mills. This difference had two important implications for the ability of the Chinese firms to withstand very strong competition and to hold their share of the market in succeeding years. Low-count yarn was spun using a more labor-intensive technology than high-count yarn, and therefore fitted the circumstances of more scarce and expensive capital and somewhat lower labor costs which the Chinese producers faced as compared with their foreign competitors. The lower-count yarn was also more readily marketed to handicraft weavers who used it as warp in combination with handspun weft to produce a coarse, long-wearing cloth much in demand in rural areas. There was a tendency, in other words, for Chinese and foreign manufacturing firms to operate in partially discrete markets, the bulk of the foreign output supplying consumers in the treaty ports and other large cities. The same pattern held in the cigarette industry where Nanyang Brothers concentrated on producing cheaper products for a different segment of consumers than BAT; in coal mining where foreign and Chinese mines did not usually operate in the same localities; and in banking where, as I noted earlier, foreign banks specialized in financing international transactions.

These observations are not intended to suggest that the modern manufacturing sector, foreign firms included, was either stagnant or not important as a base for later economic development. In fact the pre-1937 average annual rate of growth of China's industrial sector, Manchuria included, was 8 to 9 percent.[11] These plants, moreover, made important contributions to China's post 1949 economic development. Among the less obvious benefits, the inherited small-scale engineering plants in Shanghai and elsewhere contributed significantly to resolving the economic difficulties of the 1960s.[12]

What is questionable is the view that the conspicuous foreign role in the modern manufacturing sector was a primary cause of either China's overall economic backwardness or of the debilitating economic inequalities which characterized pre-1949 China. The economic consequences--with respect to both development and distribution--of whether a plant was foreign-owned or Chinese-owned were miniscule as compared with what I have already several times stated to be the primary political and psychological effects of the privileged, and in the case of modern industry sometimes dominant, foreign presence in China. Studies of pre-1949 industry, although faced with substantial data problems, show not only the impressive rate of growth cited above, but also strong evidence that Chinese-owned enterprises grew at least as fast as foreign manufacturing firms.[13] Evidence for the long-term trend in the twentieth century is scanty at best, but--excluding Manchuria after 1931 and occupied China during 1937-1945--it suggests a gradual increase for the Chinese share of capitalization and output in foreign trade and banking as well as in industry. To the extent that the traditional sector of the economy (handicraft manufacture, for example) was undermined by modern industry, the Chinese-owned modern sector, which to a large extent served the geographically and technologically discrete rural market, was primarily responsible rather than the foreign plants whose customers were more likely to be relatively well-to-do urban residents. While it is not accessible to quantitative measurement, in the long run perhaps the most important (and largely unintended) aspect of foreign manufacturing was its role in the transfer to China of modern industrial technology in the form of machinery, technical skills, and organization. This "demonstration effect" also operated in the commercial and financial sectors where Chinese foreign trading companies modeled on the foreigner began to be significant in the 1920s, and Chinese modern banks and insurance companies became increasingly important after 1911.

Foreign manufacturing firms benefited "unfairly" from their extraterritorial status, from their ability to escape some direct taxation and the especially heavy hand of Chinese officialdom, from their access to foreign capital markets, and sometimes from better management or improved technology. This privileged status, as well as their conspicuousness and hauteur, fed the burgeoning nationalism of twentieth-century China which expressed itself in "buy-Chinese" sentiments which Chinese-owned firms capitalized upon, in boycotts (for example, in 1905, 1908, 1909, 1915, 1919-1921) against both goods produced by foreign plants in China and imports, and probably in more frequent labor disputes in foreign-owned than in Chinese-owned factories. Antiimperialist sentiment was a growing reality in modern China, but it does not follow that, because nationalist propaganda pronounced it so, foreign industry in China in fact retarded China's modernization, undermined handicraft production (which contradicts the first assertion), prevented the growth of Chinese manufacturing, or exploited Chinese workers any more (or less) egregiously than native capitalists.

Transportation. In the first two decades of the twentieth century, 85 to 90 percent of China's foreign trade by value was carried in foreign flag vessels. Foreign-owned shipping also moved two-thirds of the "coast trade" between open or treaty ports, to the extent that this freight was carried in "foreign-type vessels" and thus recorded in the Maritime Customs statistics. "Inland waters navigation," i.e., steamer trade to or between places other than treaty ports, was recorded by the Customs only to the extent that dutiable cargo entered or left a treaty port. In the absence of value data, we may judge from the number of foreign (1,125) and Chinese (211) vessels registered under the Inland Steam Navigation Regulations in 1914 that this traffic, too, was dominated by foreign shipping.

That China's overseas trade was carried primarily in foreign vessels is not surprising, but cabotage, i.e., coastal and inland navigation, in international law is generally restricted to domestic carriers. Trade by foreign vessels between Chinese ports and navigation of China's rivers had been imposed upon China by the treaty powers; no reciprocal right, even in theory, was received by China. The 1858 Treaty of Tientsin authorized foreign steamer traffic to the Yangtze treaty ports, and the right once having been granted was under foreign pressure extended to China's other rivers. By the Chefoo Convention of 1876, certain "ports of call" on the Yangtze were opened at which steamers might trade under the regulations in force governing native trade. The Treaty of Shimonoseki in 1895 and a Sino-British treaty in 1897 respectively opened the upper Yangtze and the West River to foreign steamer traffic. Finally, the Chinese government yielded to repeated British demands and in the Inland Waters Steam Navigation Regulations of 1898 opened all of the inland waters of China to both Chinese and foreign steamers especially registered for that trade with the Maritime Customs.

It is impossible to assess the precise quantitative effects of foreign coastal and riverine steamer trade on traditional junks and their boatmen. Chinese government opposition to expansion of the scope of steam shipping was based in part on apprehension of possible disorders sparked by unemployed boatmen. On the other hand, on balance Chinese junks probably benefited from an expansion of total inland trade. There were countless places unreachable by steamer which were tied into the growing commerce by 500,000 junks which plied not only the rivers but also extensive networks of canals and creeks. All the qualitative indications as well as the scattered statistics available for the 1930s suggest that the junk was still the predominant means of transportation in south China in the first decades of the twentieth century. Even in 1959, only 36 percent of the total volume of goods transported in the People's Republic of China was carried by the modern transport sector; the rest primarily by junk.

Between 1903 and 1918, the major Yangtze River steamer route was shared in roughly equal proportions (with respect to both number of vessels and total tonnage) by four shipping companies: Butterfield and Swire's China Navigation Company, Jardine's Indo-China Steam Navigation Company, the Japanese Nisshin Kisen Kaisha, and the Chinese government-owned China Merchants' Steam Navigation Company. New England skippers and Scottish chief engineers predominated in the British and Chinese fleets. ("Tradition held that if you wanted the 'chief,' you just called 'Mac' down the engine-hatch and he appeared.")[14] To avoid price wars, these large lines frequently negotiated shipping rates among themselves. British and Japanese shipping dominated overall in the overseas and interport trade, the Japanese gradually drawing closer to their rival in the second decade of the century (38 percent British and 21 percent Japanese in 1910 compared to 38 percent and 29 percent respectively in 1919 of the total tonnage entered and cleared by Customs).

Transportation accounted for nearly a third (31.5 percent) of direct foreign investment in China in 1914. The bulk of this third was invested in railroads, the capitalization of the steam shipping companies being relatively small. Foreign railroad interests were a complex amalgam ranging from a fair number of unrealized railroad concessions to several major lines which were directly controlled by foreign powers. Between these two extremes were lines built entirely or in part with foreign loans under contracts which generally granted the construction of the lines to the lenders (who profited as the purchasing agents for imported materials) and, before the 1908 Tientsin-Pukow Railway Agreement, placed the management of the lines in the hands of the lenders during the period of the loan. In some cases before 1908 the foreign agencies were granted a share of the net profits until the loans were repaid. Even after 1908, most loan agreements provided for a foreign chief engineer which implied some participation by the creditors in the management of the lines so constructed.

As of 1918, out of an approximate total of 6,700 miles of railroad lines in operation, including Manchuria, only a few hundred miles of the incomplete Canton-Hankow line, the short Tientsin-Shanhaikwan section of the Peking-Mukden line, and 376 miles of the Peking-Suiyuan line had been built entirely with Chinese capital, and only the last by Chinese engineers. Foreign-owned railroads totalled 2,487 miles: Chinese Eastern Railway (Russia, 1,073 miles), South Manchuria Railway and its branches (Japan, 841 miles), Yunnan Railway (France, 289 miles), Kiachow-Tsinan Railway (Germany, Japan from 1915, 284 miles). Between 1913 and 1915 the 4,000 miles of line which constituted the Chinese Government Railways were welded into a national system, so far as accounts and statistics were concerned, with the assistance of Dr. Henry Carter Adams of the University of Michigan and the Interstate Commerce Commission who served as adviser to the Chinese government on the standardization of railroad accounts during 1913-1917. Foreign financial interests, however, in varying degrees continued to have claims on much of this mileage. By the provisions of their several loan contracts British investors had substantial control of the Peking-Mukden line (600 miles) and the Shanghai-Nanking line (204 miles); and participated in the management of the southern section of the Tientsin-Pukow line (237 miles), the Shanghai-Hangchow-Ningpo line (179 miles), and the Taokow-Chinghua line (95 miles) through British chief engineers and other personnel. A French chief engineer represented French creditors of the Cheng-tai (Shansi) Railroad (151 miles), and Belgian, Dutch, and French engineers and accountants supervised the 365 miles of the Lung-Hai line which had been completed by 1918.

I described earlier the heavily political coloring of foreign railroad investments and loans--not only in the case of such outright concessions as the Russian and Japanese lines in Manchuria but also with respect to the nominally commercial British loans in the Yangtze valley. The imperialist purposes of the several powers rather than China's economic development as an independent and desirable end from which the foreigner too might profit was what brought foreign capital into China's railroads. As glaring symbols of foreign derogation of Chinese sovereignty and territorial integrity, both the concession lines and those with heavy foreign indebtedness drew the wrath of Chinese nationalism. Foreign political interests, too, contributed to the construction of a less than optimum network of parallel lines in Manchuria. But the enormous physical capital construction contributed by the foreigner--while no study has been made of this question, it is probable that as a consequence of wars and political changes in China and abroad a substantial part of the foreign capital invested in railroads was never repaid--played a major role in providing modern transportation facilities in the northern half of China where widely separated economic regions and the absence of substantial water routes were major barriers to economic development. The Government Railways of China, even after payment of their foreign debt service, showed a profit of Ch$41 million on a total investment of Ch$522 million in 1920. This Ch$41 million is gross of any imputed interest on the Chinese government share of total investment. If that return is calculated at 5 percent, a net profit of Ch$31 million still remained. While in the warlord era, especially from 1922, profits fell and an increasingly smaller proportion came under the Peking government's control, these largely foreign-built and foreign-financed lines were an economic success.

Public Finance. In the decade 1912-1921, at least seventy mostly quite small unsecured loans and advances with a total outstanding balance of perhaps Ch$200 million in 1921 were made to various central government or provincial agencies by a very wide variety of foreign lenders. The largest were the notorious "Nishihara Loans" of 1917-1918, payments to Chinese officials by means of which Japanese interests sought to advance their claims in Manchuria and Mongolia. Given the deteriorating financial situation of the Peking government, these loans were mainly in default. The outstanding railroad loan balance of about Ch$300 million, in contrast, was regularly serviced from the income of the several lines until about 1925. But the largest part of China's foreign public indebtedness was made up by the Japanese war and indemnity loans, the Boxer Indemnity, the Crisp Loan of 1912, and the Reorganization Loan of 1913, which together represented an outstanding balance in

1921 of approximately Ch\$1,000 million.[15]   These debts were all
secured on either or both the Maritime Customs revenue and the
Salt Administration revenue, and principal and interest were paid
without interruption.

Apart from the railroad loans, these foreign funds contributed
nothing to the Chinese economy.   The indemnity loans and the Boxer
indebtedness represented a net drain while the rest were expended
for the largely unproductive administrative and military needs of the
Peking government.   Foreign lenders saw themselves as propping up
the central government or supporting some particular faction against
its rivals.   Their banks in Shanghai profited as the depositories of
the customs and salt revenues earmarked for repayment of the
secured loans, and from their control of the foreign exchange market on which Chinese silver was converted into the gold payments
stipulated in the loan agreements.   Perhaps some--certainly less
than was anticipated--political influence with Peking was secured.
Even excluding the Boxer Indemnity, annual payments of interest
and amortization on China's foreign debt in the second decade of the
century amounted to at least a quarter or a third of the revenue of
the impoverished Chinese central government.   (Financial data for
the early republic remain an unstudied morass.)

About all that can be said in favor of China's foreign indebtedness in the early republic is that on a per capita basis--perhaps
Ch\$3 in 1921--it was low by international standards.   Like the mod-
ern sector of the economy in which foreign interests were so heavily
involved, the political sway of the Peking government extended neither
very broadly nor very deeply into Chinese society.   Its economic
woes were an epiphenomenon, for which the foreigner was substantially responsible, but the specifically economic consequences of its
debility amounted to little as compared with the nationalist fury
aroused by its political fecklessness and its supine acceptance of
the presence of the privileged foreign establishment.

A dispassionate assessment of the role of the foreigner in
China's economy presents unusual difficulties.   To many Chinese
and some students of China, economic "oppression," whatever its
dimensions, stirs up greater resentments than other derogations of
China's independence or well-being.   While the distribution of political sovereignty and psychological autonomy may well be "zero-sum
games," in which some are inevitably winners and others just as

surely losers, what I have implied about the foreign economic presence in the foregoing pages is that the foreigner's economic gains, based in part on and multiplied by his privileged position, were not absolute deductions from China's economic welfare. On the contrary, China's indigenous economic modernization--the first ruptures of the "high-level equilibrium trap" which ensnared the Chinese economy at a low level of total output--began only in response to the exogenous shock of imported foreign goods and foreign manufacturing in China.[16] Trade, foreign investment in manufacturing and transportation, and the importation of technology produced absolute gains for the Chinese economy, albeit the growth of national product was slow and its social distribution questionable. In a different political context, i.e., if China had been served by an effective central government, the backward and forward linkages of foreign trade and foreign manufacture with the Chinese-owned sector of the domestic economy could undoubtedly have been greater. The foreign economic presence, however, was only one factor--and not the major one--contributing to the debility of the Chinese polity.

VI. ADVENTURERS, ADVISERS, JOURNALISTS

Although few in number, foreign adventurers, advisers, and journalists--in their relationship to the Chinese society which surrounded them and in their typical attitudes--epitomized some salient characteristics of the entire foreign presence. They were first of all highly visible, but that conspicuousness concealed the very large gap between their nominal importance and their limited real influence. For many there was also a parallel ambiguity between their service to China and their roles as nationals and in some degree agents of the foreign powers. Most characteristic perhaps were the attitudes, expressed and implied, which these foreigners shared with all the others whom I have pictured earlier--at the extreme a racism which denigrated all things Chinese, but even in the more typical and frequently unintended condescension a disposition of mind which cumulatively more profoundly affected modern China's history than all the gunboats, treaties, and imported cotton shirtings of a century. This was the real "shame" of the era of imperialism for China, and the effective personal stimulus to the nationalism which inspired the long series of attempts--from the Reform Movement of 1898, through the 1911 Revolution, the early republic under Yuan Shih-k'ai, the Nationalist Revolution of the 1920s, to the ultimately successful establishment of the People's Republic in 1949--to reintegrate Chinese society on a new basis of greater domestic equity and full international equality.

The tone of the foreigner toward China and the Chinese that I have in mind is conveyed in part by the following observation by a long-time foreign resident, himself substantially free of such asininity:

> There used to prevail a belief among the "Old China
> Hands" of the China treaty port communities that a
> study of things Chinese, including the language, dis-
> qualified the mind of the white man for any useful
> purpose. Their own knowledge of the people among
> whom they lived was often limited to what they
> learned from household servants or business asso-
> ciates; and their interest in the land was confined to
> the folklore of the Chinese pony. [1]

But this is only the negative side, the haughty indifference of the foreigner in his sheltered treaty port enclave to the China which sur-

99

rounded him. Examples of a more aggressive and insulting posture abound in the foreign press. The abusive example below was occasioned by Chinese resistance to the forcible extension of the French concession in Tientsin in October 1916.

> The Chinese agitator, particularly if he believes that he enjoys official support, is invariably willing to fight to the death for some cause that he professes to have at heart, until there is some risk that he may be taken at his word. Then he invariably beats an ignominious retreat. And unless we are greatly mistaken, this is what will happen in this case. We are familiar with the normal course of events--public and press clamor, attempts to institute a boycott, and finally, when the Power whose interests are affected, intimates that it has had enough of this tomfoolery--collapse of the whole agitation. . . . If the French Legation, after allowing sufficient time for the self-styled patriots to let off steam, intimates that this nonsense has got to cease, the great crusade for the protection of China's sovereign rights over fifteen hundred mow of land formally promised to the French authorities several months ago, will collapse as suddenly as it began. Whenever a crisis in China's foreign affairs occurs, we are treated in the Chinese press to humorous dissertations about Chinese dignity and self-respect. How such things can exist, even in the Chinese imagination, at the present moment, passes comprehension. The China of today cannot seriously expect much respect or consideration for her dignity from foreign states, because these things are only accorded to nations that are worthy of them.[2]

The literature by foreign observers of China in the 1910s and 1920s is a vast one, comparable at least to the outpouring of foreign sagacity about the People's Republic of China since 1949. Neither these publications, nor the foreign press in China, nor the abundantly available diplomatic and missionary archives have yet been systematically explored to establish a comprehensive account of the ramifications of the imperialist mind in early twentieth-century China. If I leave the subject at this point--I have brushed it lightly several times in the earlier sections of this essay--it is because it is too large to condense into the restricted pages of this particular account

of the foreign establishment. When Mao Tse-tung wrote in 1949 of
the end of "the period of modern world history in which the Chinese
and Chinese culture were looked down upon," he was pointing, I be-
lieve, to the barbed wire thread which wove together the whole fabric
of foreign imperialism in China and made it so unbearable to the
Chinese nationalism which burgeoned in the twentieth century.

It is difficult in many instances to draw a clear line between
foreign adventurers and advisers in China. And many were simultaneously journalists. The Japanese pan-Asianists in particular, who
befriended Sun Yat-sen in the first decade of the century, had an
agenda of their own to follow which only in part overlapped with the
plans of the T'ung-meng Hui.[3] After 1905 the influence in Japan of
such supporters of Sun as Miyazaki Torazō and Hirayama Shū was
much reduced and a real alliance between the Chinese nationalist
movement and Japan expansionism precluded. Yet Japanese shishi
were instrumental in arranging three loans to Sun from Mitsui in
early 1912, part of an attempt (which for the moment failed) to get
control of the Hanyehping iron and steel plant which was to be security for the loans. Japanese adventurers and the Japanese military
backed Sun's abortive insurrection in eastern Shantung in 1916.
Another Japanese, Kawashima Naniwa, was active in Manchuria in
1911, following a long residence in China which began in 1886 and
culminated with the directorship of a school (organized in Peking in
1900 and then moved to Japan) which trained some five thousand
Chinese in Japanese police methods. Kawashima returned to China
in 1911 and plotted to establish a Japanese-run puppet state in Manchuria, an effort which failed in part because it did not get the support of the more cautious Tokyo government. The failure of Sun
Yat-sen to take strong exception to the Twenty-one Demands of 1915,
making him in effect an apologist for Japanese expansionism, stemmed
as much from the continuing ambiguity of the relationship of Japanese-
inspired Pan-Asianism to Chinese hopes for reform and modernization
as from Sun's antipathy to Yuan Shih-k'ai whose discomfiture he
relished.

The late Ch'ing government and President Yuan Shih-k'ai had
their adventurers too. William Ferdinand Tyler, one of the more
colorful, left his post as an officer on Maritime Customs revenue
cruisers to fight against the Japanese at the Yalu naval battle of
September 1894 and at the siege of Weihaiwei at the beginning of
1895. In 1913, having since 1900 headed the Customs Marine Depart-

ment, Tyler handled the pay-off to the Chinese navy at Shanghai with Chinese funds made available by the Shanghai foreign banks that prevented its mutiny in support of Sun Yat-sen. Tyler left the Customs in 1918 to become an adviser to the Ministry of Communications, in which post he did little but lived well: "We took a very modest house--for Peking. It and its many courtyards covered half an acre; a series of separate bungalows--there were five of them--joined more or less by covered passages; the biggest was our drawing room with no ceiling, its massive wooden beams exposed. Mostly the windows were of paper. It took sixteen tons of coal a month to warm that house in winter--it was carried in by camels."[4]

What does one make of the likes of "general" Homer Lea (1876-1912)? Charlatan or unselfish enthusiast for the cause of Chinese freedom? His (legendary?) military exploits impressed both K'ang Yu-wei and Sun Yat-sen and the latter made him his confidential military advisor in 1911. The Australian journalist William Henry Donald (1876-1946) is somewhat easier to characterize. After a stint of Hong Kong newspaper work with The China Mail and as China correspondent for the New York Herald, in the spring of 1911 Donald sought out the republican revolutionaries. Through "Charlie" Soong in Shanghai he developed close ties with Wu T'ing-fang, Wang Chung-hui, and others, and in effect by early 1912 became the press agent to foreigners of the Sun Yat-sen group. After Yuan Shih-k'ai's assumption of the presidency, Donald continued as an adviser to Sun whom he had first met in December 1911. As the Peking correspondent of The Times of London and then as the editor of the Far Eastern Review in Shanghai, he was close to Chinese officials in and out of office, claimed (with little apparent justification) to have played a role in plotting the anti-Yuan revolt of 1915, and of course from the 1920s onward was closely associated with Chiang Kai-shek. Donald never learned more than a few words of Chinese and probably had little real influence on policy, but he was exceedingly skilled in turning out statements and official proclamations for the foreign press. In a political context in which the goodwill of the foreign establishment was perceived as a critical asset which gave advantages over one's adversaries, such advisers as Donald could occupy very pretentious positions.

John Otway Percy Bland (1863-1945) and Edmund Trelawny Backhouse (1873-1944), collaborators in writing China Under the Empress Dowager (1910) and Annals and Memoirs of the Court in Peking (1914), were two long-time British residents whose activities

on the fringes of Sino-foreign life and whose writings on China achieved
a particular notoriety. Bland entered the Customs Service in 1883
and for two years was secretary to Robert Hart. From 1896 to 1906
he served as secretary to the Municipal Council of the International
Settlement in Shanghai (contemporaries dubbed him the "uncrowned
king of Shanghai"), in which post he carried the day for the "right
of asylum" in the foreign settlements for Chinese political refugees
when he refused to hand over the reformers of 1898 to the Chinese
authorities. In 1906 Bland resigned his Shanghai position to become
agent of the British and Chinese Corporation, Limited in the negotia-
tion of four railroad loans. He was a correspondent of The Times
from 1897 to 1910, first in Shanghai and then in Peking, and before
and after his departure from China in 1916 he wrote voluminously
and often depreciatingly about Chinese life and politics (Houseboat
Days in China, 1909; Recent Events and Present Policies in China,
1912; Li Hung-chang, 1917; China, Japan and Korea, 1921; China:
The Pity of It, 1932). Bland's unalterable cynicism about Chinese
nationalism, set forth in a trenchant and lively style, represents
very well the mainstream attitudes of the predominant British segment of the foreign establishment in early twentieth-century China.

Backhouse arrived in China in 1897 as a student interpreter
attached to the British Legation and apparently acquired great skill
in translating Chinese texts--a service which he continued to render
the British government even after leaving its employ. From 1903
to 1913 he was a professor at Peking University and began the collection of some twenty-seven thousand Chinese books and manuscripts
which he later presented to the Bodleian Library at Oxford. In addition to the works written jointly with J. O. P. Bland mentioned
earlier, Backhouse collaborated with Sidney Barton, Chinese secretary to the British Legation, in revising W. C. Hillier's English-
Chinese Dictionary of Peking Colloquial (1918). Whether or not his
reputation as a scholar of China had any merit--his extensive manuscripts and papers including the draft of a large English-Chinese
dictionary were burned by the Japanese invaders in 1937--and acknowl-
edging that his influence on the British diplomats in Peking was small,
Backhouse was nevertheless a fixture on the Peking scene. His increasingly eremitic life, playing the role of the long-gowned Chinese
scholar with ever fewer foreign social contacts, was not emulated by
many, but it exemplified one small part of the foreign establishment
in China then and later.

Although he never wore Chinese dress, the later years of the career of John C. Ferguson (1866-1945) in some respects resembled that of Backhouse. Coming to China as a Methodist missionary in 1887, he presided at the beginnings of Nanking University and developed many contacts with Chinese officials. From 1897, when he took over the administration of Nanyang College (later Chiaotung University) in Shanghai, he was closely associated with Sheng Hsuan-huai, the official and entrepreneur who had founded Nanyang. Sheng helped Ferguson acquire a then small Chinese-language newspaper in Shanghai in 1899, Sin Wan Pao, which grew to be the largest of the Shanghai dailies and provided a substantial income for Ferguson and his family until he sold the paper in 1929. As Sheng's adviser, Ferguson during 1902-1911 served successively as secretary of the Ministry of Commerce, chief secretary of the Imperial Chinese Railway Administration, and foreign secretary to the Ministry of Posts and Communications. He edited the Journal of the North China Branch of the Royal Asiatic Society from 1902 to 1911, served as vice-president of the Red Cross Society of China (founded by Sheng), and was active in famine relief. With the end of the dynasty and the eclipse of Sheng Huan-huai, Ferguson returned briefly to Newton, Massachusetts, but was back again in China in 1915 at the request of the republican government, installed in a grand compound in Peking, and serving as an occasional adviser (for example, as a member of the Chinese delegation to the Washington Conference of 1921). But his main interest for the rest of his life was Chinese art. He collected discriminatingly himself (his collection was left to Nanking University), served as a buyer and consultant for the New York Metropolitan Museum and the Freer Gallery, and published extensively (Outlines of Chinese Art, 1919; Chinese Painting, 1927; Noted Porcelains of Successive Dynasties, 1931; Catalogue of the Recorded Paintings of Successive Dynasties, 1934, and Catalogue of the Recorded Bronzes of Successive Dynasties, 1939, both in Chinese; and Survey of Chinese Art, 1939). For all these pages, still more an amateur than a critical scholar, a critic of Western exploitation but not a supporter of Kuomintang nationalism in its more radical phase, Ferguson--without "going Chinese"--lived satisfyingly in that narrow margin where the foreign establishment blended into real China. Few did as well.

The brief sketches above are of course only examples intended to suggest the outlines of the larger group to which these individuals belonged. Willard D. Straight (1880-1918) is also an example, per-

haps more knowledgeable of China than most, of the concession-
hunters who, against the background of pre-World War I international
rivalries in East Asia, vied for participation in railroads, mining
and industrial projects, and loans to the Chinese government.
Straight went to China in 1901, after graduating from Cornell University, to join the Customs Service in whose employ he remained
until 1905. In 1905 he served briefly as secretary to the American
minister in Seoul, and from 1906 to 1908 as consul-general at Mukden. From November 1908 to June 1909 he was acting chief of the
Division of Far Eastern Affairs in the Department of State, before
returning to China in 1909 now as the representative of an American
banking group seeking railroad concessions in Manchuria. He was
centrally involved in the pre-1912 negotiations for an international
consortium loan to China. After leaving China in 1912, he was associated as its "Far Eastern expert" with J. P. Morgan and Company. In 1915 he became a vice-president of the American International Corporation, formed to facilitate American investment in
China. A founder of the Journal of the American Asiatic Association
(later, in a much revised format, called Asia) and of the liberal
weekly, The New Republic, Straight was certainly more genuinely
an international idealist than most of his more grubby fellow conces-
sion-hunters, but in quotidian fact in contrast to aspiration--that is,
in their immediate roles in China--they were all pretty much alike.

George Ernest Morrison (1862-1920), an Australian with an
Edinburgh M.D. who was resident correspondent of The Times in
Peking from 1897 to 1912, and (although he never bothered to learn
Chinese) as knowledgeable as any foreigner about Chinese politics
and political style, accepted the invitation of Yuan Shih-k'ai in August
1912 to become an adviser to the Chinese government. He had been
warned shortly before by the former American minister W. W. Rockhill who replied to Morrison's suggestion that Rockhill might serve
China as a foreign adviser, "What would be the role of a foreign
adviser, subject to . . . strenuous opposition to his necessary mod-
erate and conciliatory suggestions? Draw his salary and compile a
Chinese-English Dictionary, as did Walter Hillier? Such a role
would not satisfy any man who has a reputation of a life time at
stake."[5] Morrison was soon echoing Rockhill. "Here am I paid
nearly £4,000 a year and kept in complete ignorance," he wrote in
May 1913. "It quickens my determination to quit the Country as
soon as possible. And what revelations I will have to make of these
ungrateful people! Not ingratitude to me but to others. Their pusil-

lanimity. . . ." And again later, "What I want is work and no
work is being given me, that is to say no work is being entrusted
to me. These suspicious Orientals suspicious of each other especially suspicious of the foreigner are impossible to understand. Un-
willing to learn the truth they have confidence only in those base
and servile foreigners who tell them what they find pleasing to hear.
No post is worth holding under the Chinese that does not carry with
it authority and executive power. And I have neither the one nor
the other."

Morrison's own assessment of the usefulness or appropriateness
of his proposals to the Chinese government, the extent of his influence, or the degree to which he and other advisers were privy to
relevant information (they of course thought they had a "need to
know" everything, but could keep no secrets) is not to be relied
upon. He was in fact an important figure of the second rank in
Yuan's government. Morrison felt, however, that he should be more
influential than the foreign minister, perhaps even than the prime
minister, so he soon became frustrated. It didn't occur to him how
extraordinary it was that a foreigner should be as prominent as he
was in the Chinese government.[6] Among the foreign advisers to
China, only Robert Hart and, to a considerably lesser extent, his
successors as I.G. and the foreign heads of the Salt Administration
and the Post Office had both "authority and executive power." The
standards having been set by Hart, other foreigners less powerful
than he felt abused by the Chinese. It is true that many had been
taken on by the Chinese government mainly as window dressing; the
foreign establishment in China and foreign governments abroad were
to be reassured that the Chinese republic was really bent on reform
and modernization. The bruised egos, reflected in Morrison's words
above, however, signalled not just Chinese opportunism, but also an
inflated sense of self-importance which was fed by contempt for Chinese capabilities.

In the first years of the republic the foreign advisers included
Ariga Nagao, a prominent Japanese international jurist; George
Padoux, a minister in the French diplomatic service who had con-
tributed to reforming public administration in Thailand--something
he was not able to undertake in China; Henry Carter Adams, who
worked on the standardization of railroad accounts; Lieutenant-Colonel
Brissaud des Maillets, a French military adviser; Henri de Codt, a
Belgian, on problems of extraterritorial jurisdiction; William Franklin

Willoughby, who was succeeded by his twin brother Westel Woodbury
Willoughby, both noted American political scientists, as constitutional
adviser; Frank J. Goodnow, first president of the American Political
Science Association and president of Johns Hopkins University 1914-
1929, as legal adviser; and Banzai Rihachirō, military adviser to
Yuan Shih-k'ai and simultaneously agent of the Japanese general staff
--a remarkable combination, revealing of the ambiguity of the loyal-
ties of these foreign advisers, more open in Banzai's case but an
aspect of all of them and a sufficient reason for the Chinese government not bringing them any further into the center of decision making.
Like Morrison, who recruited many of them, these well-paid experts
frequently felt that they had very little to do. Whether or not all
shared in detail Morrison's deprecatory assessment of his Chinese
colleagues, they were clearly frustrated if they began with any
thoughts that they would have a role in the Chinese political system
that was consonant with their own certainty that they knew what was
best for China. Adams, as I noted earlier, did have some positive
accomplishments in the matter of railway accounting. Goodnow, who
had only enough work to keep him occupied four hours a week, was
of course used by Yuan Shih-k'ai to help justify Yuan's dictatorship
and the movement to make himself emperor. At somewhat less
eminent levels--as military instructors, in the Customs Service, as
railroad construction engineers--China's foreign employees probably
returned reasonable service for their stipends. These were not
normally positions with any policy implications.

There were other foreigners in China--short-term travelers,
students of sinology (including those at the Japanese-sponsored Tōa
Dōbun Kai, founded in 1898, who sometimes doubled as intelligence
operatives), transient overseas Chinese are examples--in these years
who might qualify as members of the foreign establishment I am de-
scribing. If I cannot give them separate treatment here, I can note
that for all of them, as for those I have already discussed, the foreign press in China was the beacon to which they turned for guidance
through the alien Chinese political and cultural landscape in which
they sojourned.

Eighty or ninety foreign-owned newspapers and periodicals cir-
culated in China in the second decade of the century. Some of these
were missionary newsletters and journals, in Chinese or a foreign
language, to which I referred earlier. A number of Chinese-language
papers were owned by foreigners; Ferguson's Sin Wan Pao I have

already mentioned; others were operated by the Japanese in south Manchuria, or were Chinese editions of such stalwarts as the Peking & Tientsin Times. A few were scholarly or professional monthlies. The most influential segment, however, was the foreign-language press in the treaty ports. Here, as elsewhere, British interests and British influence dominated. Table 8 lists the principal secular publications at the major ports and in Peking, but excluding Manchuria, as of approximately 1920.

The early foreign newspapers on the China coast were largely one-man affairs. At the beginning of the twentieth century the largest papers might have on their staffs an editor, a subeditor, three or four local reporters, correspondents in the "outports" and in Europe, all of which was supplemented by Reuters' telegrams and translations from the Chinese press. The British papers seemed to be edited on the theory that London was the news center of the world, and other parts of the British empire came next, to be followed in turn by the interests of the foreigner in China. Chinese events were treated as important only as they affected the foreigner. Founded in 1911 by Thomas F. Millard (who also established Millard's Review which became the important China Weekly Review under the editorship of J. B. Powell), the American-owned China Press departed not only from the stodgy format of the British papers which took The Times as their model (for layout if not for the quality of their contents), but also attempted to give a greater play to Chinese domestic political news. The papers with the largest circulations before World War I--which might be no more than two thousand to three thousand daily for the North-China Daily News, the leading British paper in East Asia--were the North-China Daily News founded in 1864 and its weekly edition which dated back to 1850; the Shanghai Mercury founded in 1879; the China Mail, 1845–; the South China Morning Post, 1903–; before 1917, Der Ostasiatische Lloyd founded in Shanghai in 1877; L'Echo de Chine, 1897–; the Peking & Tientsin Times, 1894–, which was widely read in the capital; and the Shanhai Nippō, established in 1904 as a successor to an earlier Japanese publication dating back to 1890.

How brightly and how briefly shone the beacon. The Peking & Tientsin Times--"The leading daily newspaper of Northern China, British Owned and British Edited. Entirely independent in its views and criticisms"; so its advertising blurb went. And, "The North-China Daily News writes the history of China. It records the pulse

TABLE 8

PRINCIPAL SECULAR FOREIGN PERIODICALS IN CHINA

Place of Publication	Title of Periodical	Nationality	Frequency
Peking	North China Standard	Japanese	Daily
	Journal de Pékin	French	Daily
Tientsin	Peking and Tientsin Times	British	Daily
	China Illustrated Review	British	Weekly ed. of the above
	North China Daily Mail	British	Daily
	China Advertiser	Japanese	Daily
	Tenshin Nichi-nichi Shimbun	Japanese	Daily
	L'Echo de Tientsin	French	Daily
	North China Star	American	Daily
Hankow	Central China Post	British	Daily
Shanghai	North-China Daily News	British	Daily
	North-China Herald	British	Weekly ed. of the above
	Shanghai Mercury	British	Daily
	Shanghai Times	British	Daily
	Shanghai Sunday Times	British	Weekly
	Finance and Commerce	British	Weekly
	New China Review	British	Monthly
	Shanhai Nippō	Japanese	Daily
	L'Echo de Chine	French	Daily
	China Press	American	Daily
	Evening Star	American	Daily
	China Weekly Review	American	Weekly
	Far Eastern Review	American	Monthly
Hong Kong	Hongkong Daily Press	British	Daily
	South China Morning Post	British	Daily
	Hongkong Telegraph	British	Daily
	China Mail	British	Daily

of its politics; it reports the conditions of its finance and markets; and it chronicles the daily doings of its people." For the business, consular, and missionary offices of the treaty ports the foreign press not only interpreted China in its own special light, as the inevitable but froward beneficiary of the foreign presence which sought to modernize it, reform it, convert it, tame its nationalism, and incorporate it into the European international system. In an important degree it also wove that disparate presence, whose many aspects I have touched upon, into a self-conscious and conservative "foreign establishment," each component--although sometimes begrudgingly--linked arm and arm with its collaborator to form a mighty weight pressing upon a China now departed from the grandeur of its imperial past but still unable to move with certainty into an autonomous future.

*　　*　　*

"It's extraordinary," a fellow sinologist recently wrote to me, "how much we talk about the foreign presence and how little has been written recounting its dimensions." While I have provided little new information in detail not previously within the ken of specialists, the preparation of a rough working drawing of the foreign establishment in early republican China may encourage other efforts to fill a large gap in the literature on China's modern history. The "talk about the foreign presence" to which my correspondent referred consists in substantial part of conventional ascription of China's twentieth-century ills to a looming but ill-defined nemesis christened "imperialism." I am myself prone to both the concept and the word --it does appear on occasion in the foregoing pages--but I am at the same time singularly uncomfortable with derivative accounts which draw selectively upon the data furnished by economic historians, myself included, to assert that the principal face of foreign imperialism in China was economic exploitation.

What I have implied in my working drawing is, first, that the foreigner and his works occupied only a secondary place in the largely autochthonous design of China's twentieth-century history. But what is secondary is not therefore unimportant, in particular as it gave rise to modern Chinese nationalism--the ideology and the organization (in successive guises) which constitute the motive power and the primary structure of that history.

The second inference to be drawn from my blueprint is that the specific economic consequences of imperialism--that is, the measurable results of foreign trade, banking, loans, and manufacture--were at worst ambiguous ones for the Chinese economy. What made foreign economic penetration significant was what it shared with the foreign establishment as a whole: an invasion of China's sovereignty which derogated the autonomy not only of an abstract polity but also, more critically, the autonomy of particular and individual Chinese who apprehended and reacted to the intruding foreign presence. Indeed, a similar comment is applicable to each aspect of the foreign establishment that I have sketched in this essay. The immediate and observable effects on China of territorial enclaves; soldiers and sailors; ministers and consuls; missionaries; traders and bankers; officials of the customs, post office, and salt administration; adventurers, advisers, and journalists were in each case miniscule as compared with the interplay of the domestic ideological, political, and military forces which struggled for modern China. But superimposed upon the narrow measurable consequences of the separate facets of the foreign presence was a common propensity for self-inflation, a derision of Chinese culture and capabilities, even an egregious certainty that what the foreigners did was best for China as well as for themselves. The typical foreign attitude served to reinforce and exaggerate among patriotic Chinese the sense of threat already occasioned by the concrete foreign presence.

Even if the several guises of imperialism had been relatively benign, which on balance they were not, Chinese nationalism, from the late-Ch'ing reformers to Mao Tse-tung, could not apprehend them apart from the aggressive foreign egoism of the semi-colonial era. No cool description such as one who writes history might undertake was possible for those who experienced the ignominious treatment to which their nation and themselves were subjected by the "lords of humankind." Imperialism then, as the midwife of Chinese nationalism, must be understood to encompass not only the foreign institutions and actions which I have described, but also the heightened Chinese apprehension of them--partly myth to be sure if one stays with the documented record, but a powerful impetus to political mobilization precisely because it fired emotions as well as imported textiles, marketed cigarettes and preached in street chapels.

NOTES

I. Territory, People, Extraterritoriality, Armed Force

1. James L. Hutchison, China Hand (Boston: Lothrop, Lee, and Shepard, 1936), p. 20.

2. Ibid., p. 236.

3. Imperial Japanese Government Railways, An Official Guide to Eastern Asia, Vol. IV, China (Tokyo, 1915), and C. E. Darwent, Shanghai, A Handbook for Travellers and Residents (Shanghai: Kelly & Walsh, n.d.) provide interesting details.

4. The agreements covering these leases may be found in John V. A. MacMurray, Treaties and Agreements with and Concerning China, 1894-1919, 2 vols. (New York: Oxford University Press, 1921), 1:112-131, 152-158.

5. See B. A. Romanov, Russia in Manchuria (1892-1906), trans. Susan W. Jones (Ann Arbor, 1952).

6. See Ronald S. Suleski, "Manchuria Under Chang Tso-lin" (Ph.D. diss., The University of Michigan, 1974).

7. See John E. Schrecker, Imperialism and Chinese Nationalism: Germany in Shantung (Cambridge: Harvard University Press, 1971).

8. See L. K. Young, British Policy in China, 1895-1902 (Oxford: Oxford University Press, 1970).

9. China, Inspectorate General of Customs, Decennial Reports . . . , 1902-1911, 2 vols. (Shanghai, 1913), 2:354-355; Decennial Reports . . . , 1912-1921, 2 vols. (Shanghai, 1924), 2:450-451.

10. Carroll Lunt, ed., The China Who's Who (Foreign) (Shanghai-- I have seen editions for 1922 and 1925), provides brief biographies based on questionnaires returned by foreign residents.

11. John Carter Vincent, The Extraterritorial System in China: Final
     Phase (Cambridge: Harvard University Press, 1970), p. 26.

12. The China Year Book, 1919-20, p. 333; The China Year Book, 1923,
     pp. 603-604; Conference on the Limitation of Armament, Washing-
     ton, November 12, 1921 – February 6, 1922, 2 vols. (Washington:
     U.S. Government Printing Office, 1922), pp. 988-998.

II. Ministers and Consuls

 1. Daniele Varè, Laughing Diplomat (New York: Doubleday, Doran
     & Co., 1938), p. 128.

 2. Ibid., p. 120.

 3. Sir Meyrick Hewlitt, Forty Years in China (London: Macmillan,
     1943), p. 35.

 4. H. B. Morse wrote, "The Legation Quarter may be considered
     as the provision of a defensible fortress in the heart of the
     capital of a hostile Power--for which purpose it was much too
     large; or as the happy grasping of the opportunity to provide
     spacious quarters for the diplomatic representatives of the
     Powers, in park-like surroundings, free from the old-time
     insanitary conditions, and at the cost of China--and in that
     case it was not justified. " The International Relations of the
     Chinese Empire, 3 vols. (London: Longmans, 1910-18), 3:355.

 5. Charles Denby, China and Her People, 2 vols. (Boston: L. C.
     Page, 1906), 1:34-35.

 6. Cyril Pearl, Morrison of China (Sydney: Angus & Robertson
     Ltd., 1967), p. 86, summarizing G. E. Morrison's impres-
     sions as noted in his unpublished diaries.

 7. Varè, Laughing Diplomat, p. 88.

 8. Hewlett, Forty Years in China, p. 4.

 9. Varè, Laughing Diplomat, p. 88.

10.   Paul S. Reinsch, An American Diplomat in China (Garden City,
       N.Y.: Doubleday, Page & Co., 1922), p. 20.

11.   Varè, Laughing Diplomat, p. 92.

12.   Denby, China and Her People, 1:91.

13.   Ibid., 1:99.

14.   John A. Moore, Jr., "The Chinese Consortiums and American-
       China Policy, 1909-1917" (Ph.D. diss., Claremont Graduate
       School, 1972), pp. 18-31.

III. Missionaries

1.   China Continuation Committee, The Christian Occupation of
       China: A General Survey of the Numerical Strength and Geo-
       graphical Distribution of the Christian Forces in China Made
       by the Special Committee on Survey and Occupation, China
       Continuation Committee, 1918-1921 (Shanghai, 1922), Introduc-
       tion, p. 3.

2.   Most of the numerical data below are from the volume cited
       in the previous note. Information about the Roman Catholic
       "occupation" is from Kenneth Scott Latourette, A History of
       Christian Missions in China (New York: Macmillan, 1929).

3.   Of the number of "missionaries" reported, at any one time as
       many as one-sixth of the foreign workers might be out of China
       on furlough, approximately one-twelfth newly arrived and en-
       gaged primarily in language study, and many of the married
       women occupied only part-time with religious work. The num-
       ber of full-time effectives, therefore, may be estimated at
       two-thirds of the totals reported.

4.   Sidney A. Forsythe, An American Missionary Community in
       China, 1895-1905 (Cambridge: Harvard University Press,
       1971), Forward, p. vii.

5.   See Stuart Creighton Miller, "Ends and Means: Missionary
       Justification of Force in Nineteenth Century China," in The

Missionary Enterprise in China and America, ed. John K.
Fairbank (Cambridge: Harvard University Press, 1974),
pp. 249-282.

6.   See Jessie Gregory Lutz, China and the Christian Colleges,
      1850-1950 (Ithaca: Cornell University Press, 1971).

IV. Maritime Customs, Post Office, Salt Administration

1.   Hu Sheng, Imperialism and Chinese Politics (Peking: Foreign
      Languages Press, 1955), p. 66.   Hu's book was withdrawn
      from circulation in the 1960s.

2.   Hart, a native of Northern Ireland and graduate of the Queen's
      University in Belfast, left the British Consular service in 1859
      to become deputy Customs commissioner at Canton.   From
      June 1861 until his substantive appointment as I.G. in Novem-
      ber 1863 to replace the dismissed Horatio N. Lay, he was one
      of two "Officiating Inspectors General." Hart left Peking for
      England in May 1908, and while he formally retained the title
      of I.G. until his death in September 1911, his departure marked
      the effective terminus of his domination of the Customs. Robert
      E. Bredon (1846-1918) served as acting I.G. from April 1908
      to April 1910, to be succeeded in turn during 1910-1911 by
      Francis A. Aglen (1869-1932) who became I.G. at Hart's death
      and served until dismissed in January 1927.   See Stanley F.
      Wright, Hart and the Chinese Customs (Belfast: Wm. Mullan
      & Son, 1950); John K. Fairbank, et al., eds., The Inspector
      General in Peking: Letters of Robert Hart, Chinese Maritime
      Customs, 1868-1907, 2 vols. (Cambridge: Harvard University
      Press, 1976); and China, Inspectorate General of Customs,
      Documents Illustrative of the Origin, Development and Activities
      of the Chinese Customs Service, 7 vols. (Shanghai: Inspectorate
      General of Customs, 1937-1940).

3.   Quoted in Wright, Hart and the Chinese Customs, p. 541.

4.   By Article VI of the Boxer Protocol, the revenues of the Native
      Customs at the treaty ports and inside a fifty-li radius were
      hypothecated to the service of the Indemnity and these collec-
      torates placed under the administration of the Maritime Customs.

Hart assumed nominal control in November 1901, but in practice until 1911 the Indemnity payments due from the Native Customs were largely met from other provincial appropriations.
Complete control over the Native Customs within fifty li of the
treaty ports was asserted only after the Revolution of 1911 dis-
rupted the remittance of provincial quotas for the Indemnity
service, a circumstance which alarmed foreign bondholders.
See Stanley F. Wright, China's Customs Revenue since the
Revolution of 1911, 3rd ed. (Shanghai: Inspectorate General
of Customs, 1935), pp. 181-182.

5. See Stanley F. Wright, China's Struggle for Tariff Autonomy:
   1843-1938 (Shanghai: Kelly & Walsh, 1938).

6. The inward transit pass privilege was extended to Chinese
   nationals by the Chefoo Convention of 1876 (actually imple-
   mented from 1880) but Peking demurred until 1896 before
   conceding the outward transit pass to Chinese merchants.
   For a detailed guide to Customs practices, see China, The
   Maritime Customs, Handbook of Customs Procedure at Shanghai (Shanghai: Kelly & Walsh, 1921).

7. Quoted in Wright, Hart and the Chinese Customs, p. 262.

8. Wright, Hart and the Chinese Customs, p. 903.

9. Hsiao Ling-lin, China's Foreign Trade Statistics, 1864-1949
   (Cambridge: Harvard University Press, 1974), pp. 201-223.

10. I.G. Circular No. 1732 (Second Series), Documents Illustra-
    tive . . . of the Chinese Customs Service, Vol. 2: Inspector
    General's Circulars, 1893-1910, p. 709.

11. Semi-Official Circular No. 29, Documents Illustrative . . . of
    the Chinese Customs Service, Vol. 3: Inspector General's Cir-
    culars, 1911 to 1923, p. 504.

12. Statement by Japanese delegation to the Washington Conference,
    quoted in Westel W. Willoughby, Foreign Rights and Interests
    in China, 2 vols. (Baltimore: Johns Hopkins Press, rev. and
    enl. ed., 1927), p. 887.

13. See Ying-wan Cheng, Postal Communication in China and Its
     Modernization, 1860-1896 (Cambridge: Harvard University
     Press, 1970).

14. For Dane's reforms, see S. A. M. Adshead, The Modernization
     of the Chinese Salt Administration, 1900-1920 (Cambridge: Har-
     vard University Press, 1970).

15. Japan, Gaimushō, Ajia-kyoku, Shina yōhei gaikoku-jin jimmeirok
     [List of foreign employees of China] (Tokyo, 1925).

V. Economic Interests

 1. Albert Feuerwerker, The Chinese Economy, 1912-1949 (Ann
     Arbor: University of Michigan Center for Chinese Studies,
     1968); Carl Riskin, "Surplus and Stagnation in Modern China,"
     in China's Modern Economy in Historical Perspective, ed.
     Dwight H. Perkins (Stanford: Stanford University Press, 1975),
     pp. 49-84.

 2. The statistical data cited below were derived mainly from the
     following sources: Yen Chung-p'ing, Chung-kuo chin-tai ching-
     chi shih t'ung-chi tzu-liao hsüan-chi [Selected statistical ma-
     terials on modern Chinese economic history] (Peking, 1955);
     Chi-ming Hou, Foreign Investment and Economic Development
     in China, 1840-1937 (Cambridge: Harvard University Press,
     1965); and Hsiao, China's Foreign Trade Statistics, 1864-1949.

 3. Albert Feuerwerker, The Chinese Economy, ca. 1870-1911
     (Ann Arbor: University of Michigan Center for Chinese Studies,
     1969), pp. 56-57.

 4. G. C. Allen and Audrey G. Donnithorne, Western Enterprise
     in Far Eastern Economic Development: China and Japan
     (London: George Allen & Unwin, 1954) provides a detailed
     account.

 5. Ralph W. Hidy and Muriel E. Hidy, Pioneering in Big Business,
     1882-1911 (New York: Harper, 1955), p. 552.

6. See Sherman G. Cochran, "Big Business in China: Sino-American Rivalry in the Tobacco Industry, 1890-1930" (Ph.D. diss., Yale University, 1975), on BAT in China.

7. Andrea Lee McElderry, Shanghai Old-Style Banks (Ch'ien-chuang), 1800-1935 (Ann Arbor: University of Michigan Center for Chinese Studies, 1976), pp. 21-22.

8. See Hsien K'o, Chin pai nien lai ti-kuo chu-i tsai Hua yin-hang fa-hsing chih-pi kai-k'uang [The issue of bank notes in China by imperialist banks in the past 100 years] (Peking, 1958), passim.

9. C. S. Chen, "Profits of British Bankers from Chinese Loans, 1895-1914," Tsing Hua Journal of Chinese Studies, New Series, 5.1 (July 1965), pp. 107-120.

10. John K. Chang, Industrial Development in Pre-Communist China: A Quantitative Analysis (Chicago: Aldine, 1969), p. 55.

11. Ibid., pp. 70-74.

12. See Thomas G. Rawski, "The Growth of Producer Industries, 1900-1971," in China's Modern Economy in Historical Perspective, ed. Perkins, pp. 203-234.

13. Chi-ming Hou, Foreign Investment, pp. 138-141.

14. Esson M. Gale, Salt for the Dragon: A Personal History of China, 1908-45 (East Lansing: Michigan State College Press, 1953), p. 66.

15. Hsü I-sheng, Chung-kuo chin-tai wai chai shih t'ung-chi tzu-liao, 1853-1927 [Statistics of China's modern foreign loans, 1853-1927] (Peking, 1962), and The China Year Book, 1923, pp. 713-727, 744-748.

16. See Robert F. Dernberger, "The Role of the Foreigner in China's Economic Development, 1840-1949," in China's

Modern Economy in Historical Perspective, ed. Perkins,
pp. 19-47.

VI. Adventurers, Advisers, Journalists

1.   Gale, Salt for the Dragon, p. 24.

2.   Quoted in Ellen La Motte, Peking Dust (New York: The
      Century Co., 1919), pp. 98-99 from a "semi-official"
      English newspaper in Peking, probably the Peking & Tientsin
      Times.

3.   For a record of Japanese "adventurers," consult Tōa Dōbunkai,
      comp., Tai Shi Kaikoroku [Memoirs of activities in China],
      2 vols. (Tokyo, 1968; reprint of 1936 ed.).

4.   William Ferdinand Tyler, Pulling Strings in China (London:
      Constable, 1929), p. 272.

5.   Quoted in Pearl, Morrison of China, p. 257. The quotations
      that follow appear on pp. 278-279.

6.   See Ernest P. Young, The Presidency of Yuan Shih-k'ai:
      Liberalism and Dictatorship in Early Republican China
      (Ann Arbor: University of Michigan Press, 1976).

MICHIGAN PAPERS IN CHINESE STUDIES

No. 1. The Chinese Economy, 1912-1949, by Albert Feuerwerker.

No. 2. The Cultural Revolution: 1967 in Review, four essays by Michel Oksenberg, Carl Riskin, Robert Scalapino, and Ezra Vogel.

No. 3. Two Studies in Chinese Literature, by Li Chi and Dale Johnson.

No. 4. Early Communist China: Two Studies, by Ronald Suleski and Daniel Bays.

No. 5. The Chinese Economy, ca. 1870-1911, by Albert Feuerwerker.

No. 6. Chinese Paintings in Chinese Publications, 1956-1968: An Annotated Bibliography and an Index to the Paintings, by E. J. Laing.

No. 7. The Treaty Ports and China's Modernization: What Went Wrong? by Rhoads Murphey.

No. 8. Two Twelfth Century Texts on Chinese Painting, by Robert J. Maeda.

No. 9. The Economy of Communist China, 1949-1969, by Chu-yuan Cheng.

No. 10. Educated Youth and the Cultural Revolution in China, by Martin Singer.

No. 11. Premodern China: A Bibliographical Introduction, by Chun-shu Chang.

No. 12. Two Studies on Ming History, by Charles O. Hucker.

No. 13. Nineteenth Century China: Five Imperialist Perspectives, selected by Dilip Basu, edited by Rhoads Murphey.

No. 14. Modern China, 1840-1972: An Introduction to Sources and Research Aids, by Andrew J. Nathan.

No. 15. Women in China: Studies in Social Change and Feminism, edited by Marilyn B. Young.

No. 16. An Annotated Bibliography of Chinese Painting Catalogues and Related Texts, by Hin-cheung Lovell.

No. 17. China's Allocation of Fixed Capital Investment, 1952-1957, by Chu-yuan Cheng.

No. 18. Health, Conflict, and the Chinese Political System, by David M. Lampton.

No. 19. Chinese and Japanese Music-Dramas, edited by J. I. Crump and William P. Malm.

No. 20. Hsin-lun (New Treatise) and Other Writings by Huan T'an (43 B.C.-28 A.D.), translated by Timoteus Pokora.

No. 21. Rebellion in Nineteenth-Century China, by Albert Feuerwerker.

No. 22. Between Two Plenums: China's Intraleadership Conflict, 1959-1962, by Ellis Joffe.

No. 23. "Proletarian Hegemony" in the Chinese Revolution and the Canton Commune of 1927, by S. Bernard Thomas.

No. 24. Chinese Communist Materials at the Bureau of Investigation Archives, Taiwan, by Peter Donovan, Carl E. Dorris, and Lawrence Sullivan.

No. 25. Shanghai Old-Style Banks (Ch'ien-chuang), 1800-1935, by Andrea Lee McElderry.

No. 26. The Sian Incident: A Pivotal Point in Modern Chinese History, by Tien-wei Wu.

No. 27. State and Society in Eighteenth-Century China: The Ch'ing Empire in Its Glory, by Albert Feuerwerker.

No. 28. Intellectual Ferment for Political Reforms in Taiwan, 1971-1973, by Mab Huang.

No. 29. The Foreign Establishment in China in the Early Twentieth Century, by Albert Feuerwerker.

MICHIGAN ABSTRACTS OF CHINESE AND JAPANESE WORKS ON CHINESE HISTORY

No. 1. The Ming Tribute Grain System, by Hoshi Ayao, translated by Mark Elvin.

No. 2. Commerce and Society in Sung China, by Shiba Yoshinobu, translated by Mark Elvin.

No. 3. Transport in Transition: The Evolution of Traditional Shipping in China, translations by Andrew Watson.

No. 4. Japanese Perspectives on China's Early Modernization: A Bibliographical Survey, by K. H. Kim.

No. 5. The Silk Industry in Ch'ing China, by Shih Min-hsiung, translated by E-tu Zen Sun.

NONSERIES PUBLICATION

Index to the "Chan-kuo Ts'e," by Sharon Fidler and J. I. Crump. A companion volume to the Chan-kuo Ts'e, translated by J. I. Crump (Oxford: Clarendon Press, 1970).

Michigan Papers and Abstracts available from:
Center for Chinese Studies
The University of Michigan
Lane Hall (Publications)
Ann Arbor, MI 48109 USA

Prepaid Orders Only
write for complete price listing